STEP BY STEP THROUGH THE NEW TESTAMENT

– LEADER GUIDE –

RICK MITCHELL

LifeWay Press®
Nashville, Tennessee

© 1991 • LifeWay Press®

Ninth printing December 2005
Revised 2000

No part of this book may be reproduced or transmitted in any form or by any means, electronic or mechanical, including photocopying and recording, or by any information storage or retrieval system, except as may be expressly permitted in writing by the publisher. Requests for permission should be addressed in writing to LifeWay Press®; One LifeWay Plaza; Nashville, TN 37234-0175.

ISBN 0-7673-2621-0

This book is the text for course CG-0104
in the subject area Bible Studies in the Christian Growth Study Plan.

Dewey Decimal Classification: 221
Subject Heading: BIBLE.OLD TESTAMENT

About the Author:
Rick Mitchell is a graduate of the University of Alabama and the New Orleans Baptist Theological Seminary (MDiv). Rick became involved in small-group disciple making in 1984, and pastored for 20 years in Alabama, Louisiana, and Mississippi. He now serves as a bi-vocational minister and consultant to churches. Rick is employed as a corporate consultant doing leadership development, employee and executive assessment, and seminar development and training. He resides in Tuscaloosa, Alabama, with his wife, Carol, and their daughters, Jennifer and Rachel.

Cover Design: Jon Rodda
Cover Illustration: Stefano Vitale

Unless otherwise indicated, Scripture quotations are from: The Holy Bible.
New International Version, copyright © 1973, 1978, 1984 by International Bible Society.

To order additional copies of this resource: WRITE LifeWay Church Resources Customer Service; One LifeWay Plaza; Nashville, TN 37234-0113; FAX order to (615) 251-5933; PHONE (800) 458-2772; ORDER ONLINE at *www.lifeway.com;* or VISIT the LifeWay Christian Store serving you.

Printed in the United States of America

Leadership and Adult Publishing
LifeWay Church Resources
One LifeWay Plaza
Nashville, TN 37234-0175

Table of Contents

	Author	2
	Life Enrollment/Attendance Form	4
	Introduction and Administrative Guide	5
INTRODUCTORY SESSION	Introducing *Step by Step Through the New Testament*	12
GROUP SESSION 1	God and the New Covenant	14
	A Chronology of Events, Miracles, and Parable in Jesus' Life and Ministry	17
GROUP SESSION 2	Introduction to the Gospels	19
GROUP SESSION 3	The Gospel of Matthew	22
GROUP SESSION 4	The Gospel of Mark	26
GROUP SESSION 5	The Gospel of Luke	29
GROUP SESSION 6	The Gospel of John	32
GROUP SESSION 7	The Book of Acts, Part I	36
GROUP SESSION 8	The Book of Acts, Part II	40
GROUP SESSION 9	The Writings of Paul, Part I	44
GROUP SESSION 10	The Writings of Paul, Part II	47
GROUP SESSION 11	The Writings of Paul, Part III	51
GROUP SESSION 12	The General Letters	55
GROUP SESSION 13	The Book of Revelation	58
	Unit Review Quizzes	61

LIFE Enrollment/Attendance

Course Title _____

Leader _____

Name	Session Date (Check Attendance)												
	1	2	3	4	5	6	7	8	9	10	11	12	13
1													
2													
3													
4													
5													
6													
7													
8													
9													
10													

* Report weekly attendance to your Discipleship Training Director or general secretary.

** You have permission to reproduce this form for use with your LIFE course small group.

Introduction and Administrative Guide

SMALL-GROUP DISCIPLING
The Small-Group Discipling Process
The purpose of a discipleship group is to aid in the spiritual growth of each member. Members of a discipleship group enter into a discipling relationship with the leaders and with one another. Christian discipleship involves the redirection of one's life in obedience to Christ so the disciple can more closely follow Him and more nearly become like Him. One of the best contexts in which this may occur is in a small group where group members help one another grow as Christ's disciples. As the leader you should be the best possible model. Often the group members will learn as much from their sharing with one another and by your example as from what they study.

The group relationship gives us insight as we learn. It also provides us support as we seek to redirect our lives under the lordship of Christ. Group members need to feel a responsibility for one another and commit to mutually helping one another.

Size of Groups for Effective Learning
Jesus preached to large crowds, but He did most of His discipleship training with a group of 12. He was even more intimate with three of His disciples who would be key leaders in the early church. You need to provide a learning environment where God can do His best work in the lives of group members. Being in a small group makes it easier to ask questions, share personal experiences, and pray intimately with one another. Eight to ten members is the best size for a group of this nature. If more persons are interested in this study, it would be wise to provide for several small groups in order to create the best possible learning environment.

A Word About Multiplication
"The things you have heard me say in the presence of many witnesses entrust to reliable men who will also be qualified to teach others" (2 Tim. 2:2). Our goal is to make disciples who will make disciples. Christian discipleship is not complete until the disciple is helping others to be disciples. Watch for persons who show potential for becoming leaders themselves. Give them opportunities to share in leading part of a session. If you have to be absent for a session, enlist one of these to serve as leader in your place.

Strive for quality instead of quantity. Starting small and growing is better than starting big and failing. Commit yourself to doing the kind of quality discipling that requires patience, hard work, accountability, and vision. The long-term benefit will be worth it. You will witness the infusion of renewed spiritual life and vitality into every area of the church as God grows and matures His people.

AN OVERVIEW OF *STEP BY STEP THROUGH THE NEW TESTAMENT*
For an introduction to the course, read the introduction in the member book (pp. 5-6) before you continue reading this overview.

Step by Step Through the New Testament is a 13-session survey of the New Testament. The basic goal of the course is to offer adult Christians an overview of the 27 books of the New Testament and to help them understand how the books relate to each other and to our Savior. However, *Step by Step Through the New Testament* is not just a book for reading. It is part of a learning system designed to teach the content material in such a way that will help people move into a deeper relationship with God.

Step by Step Through the New Testament is a preparation for ministry course. It directly relates to the ministries of teaching and preaching and will be of immediate benefit to church leaders responsible for the teaching and preaching ministries of your church (for example, Sunday School teachers, church members involved in Bible study, serious Bible students, pastor, minister of education, and other staff ministers). Members will come away from the course with a broad grasp of the people, places, themes, and message of the New Testament. However, *Step by Step Through the New Testament* will also provide a dynamic benefit to other church leaders and church members who wish to equip themselves for a broader and deeper ministry in the church.

The LIFE Learning System
Step by Step Through the New Testament and other LIFE courses are offered as a part of the Discipleship Training provided by your church. If your church does not have a regular member training program for disciples, you

still can offer the course. In fact, some churches are using LIFE courses to start or revitalize their training of disciples. LIFE (Lay Institute for Equipping) is a self-study system designed to equip adult Christians with knowledge and skills in basic ministry areas. The courses are taught using an interactive learning model. For maximum benefits, every element of the learning system should be utilized. Participants should complete each daily study on their own. They then meet weekly in a small group (eight to ten people is best) to review, discuss questions that arise, share personal experiences and insights, and apply the truths to life. *Step by Step Through the New Testament* is part of that system.

The Uniqueness of *Step by Step Through the New Testament*

If you have already studied *Step by Step Through the Old Testament*, you have learned that God the Father is the author, subject, and focal point of the Old Testament. This study will help you know more about God's new covenant (testament). You will learn of the life and ministry of Jesus, God's Son, through whom God chose to reveal Himself fully and finally. You will make a close examination of the major people, places, themes, and events related to Jesus and His life (the four gospels). You also will learn of the church He founded and left to finish His work, and you will be reminded of the present ministry of God's Spirit in the world (Acts through Revelation). Think of this fact—23 of the 27 books of our New Testament were written to and about the church of Jesus Christ! Finally, you should experience the voice of God's Spirit speaking to you personally as you study the New Testament. The Bible is God's Word, and God uses His Word today to bless, strengthen, and guide His people. Experience spiritual renewal in your own life as you let Him speak to you through His record of our Savior's life and ministry.

Step by Step Through the New Testament is designed to be an informational as well as inspirational overview offering a framework of knowledge for church teachers and leaders as they seek to equip and lead God's people. Any Christian will benefit from studying *Step by Step Through the New Testament*. However, those who teach and lead Bible study make up the primary audience for this course. Pastors who need introductory training or simply want an intensive refresher course in New Testament make up another target audience for this course.

How to Use This Guide

This leader's guide is designed to assist you in preparing for and conducting the small-group sessions each week. The following material will guide you in preparing for the course, enlisting participants, and preparing for the small-group sessions.

1. If you have not already done so, read thoroughly the introduction to the course in the member's book.
2. Next, finish reading this course administrative guide (pp. 5-11).
3. Using the instructions in this guide, make a list of and begin gathering necessary supplies and extra resources you may need.
4. Use a calendar to outline a time frame for the course. Plan for a period of about 16 weeks.

GETTING GROUPS STARTED

Decide on the Number of Groups Needed

Work with the pastor, Discipleship Training director, or others to determine how many individuals in your church want to study this course at this time. Any adult who already has trusted Jesus Christ as Lord and Savior will benefit from this study. Survey your church membership to determine the number of persons interested in a study of the New Testament. It is possible that people outside your church membership (for example, spouse of a member) or someone who has not yet trusted Jesus as Lord and Savior may wish to join the group in order to learn more about the New Testament or more about Jesus. As mentioned earlier, you will need one group for every 10 to 12 members.

Order Resources

Necessary resources should be ordered for the course eight to ten weeks prior to the first session. Course materials may be ordered on the Undated Resources Order Form, or by calling LifeWay Christian Resources. Allow time for processing and shipping your order—remember that leaders need time to prepare for the introductory session and to enlist participants. Though you may not enlist participants until later, you can estimate the quantity needed by ordering eight to ten member books and one leader guide for each small group. Resources include:

- *Step by Step Through the New Testament (Member Book)* (ISBN: 0-8054-9946-6)
- *Step by Step Through the New Testament Leader Guide* (ISBN 0-7673-2621-0)

A similar set of resources is available for *Step by Step Through the Old Testament*.
- *Step by Step Through the Old Testament* (Member Book) (ISBN 0-7673-2619-9)
- *Step by Step Through the Old Testament Leader Guide* (ISBN 0-7673-2620-2)

Orders or order inquiries may be sent to
- LifeWay Church Resources Customer Service One LifeWay Plaza; Nashville, TN 37234-0113;
- FAX order to (615) 251-5933;
- PHONE 1-800-458-2772;
- EMAIL to *customerservice@lifeway.com;*
- ORDER ONLINE at *www.lifeway.com;* or
- VISIT the LifeWay Christian Store serving you.

Enlist Leaders

Each group should have at least one leader. The primary role of leaders of *Step by Step Through the New Testament* is that of facilitator. As such, they are to be role models and catalysts for learning. Pray that God will help you identify those persons that He wants to lead the groups. These leaders should be spiritually growing Christians and active church members. Leaders should have teachable spirits, ability to relate well to people, a commitment to keep confidential information private, and a willingness to spend the time necessary to prepare for the sessions.

Look for people who possess skills for leading small-group learning experiences. They should be interested in developing disciples. Alumni of *MasterLife: Discipleship Training* could make excellent group leaders since they have experienced the discipling process. To sum up some of the requirements for leaders, they should
- be dedicated, faithful Christians.
- be role models in their knowledge and practice of Bible teachings.
- love people and enjoy helping them grow in Christ.

Explore with your pastor the possibility of his leading the first group. Having your pastor lead the first study offers several advantages.
- Pastoral leadership attaches importance to the study in the eyes of church members.
- The pastor is afforded an opportunity to share with church members in a unique, small-group setting not available in regular worship sessions.
- The pastor's spiritual growth is enhanced.
- Leaders for future groups can be identified and benefit from the modeling done by the pastor as he leads the initial study.

Enlist Participants

Whom should you enlist? Here are some suggestions that will help you know where to look for prospective group members.
- Church leaders and church program teachers.
- New Christians who have completed *Survival Kit for New Christians.*
- Persons who have joined your church from other denominations.
- Members who want to grow in Christ.
- Potential leaders.
- MasterLife alumni.

How should you enlist group members? Use these suggestions as guidelines for enlistment efforts.
- Pray for God to lead you and them.
- Promote the course as you would other study opportunities.
- Make a personal contact before a person is enlisted as a group member. Sit down with the person and explain the expectations, requirements, anticipated results, and materials costs of the course.

What are the requirements? Each participant should have clear understanding of the following requirements.
- Individual study of about 30-60 minutes a day for five days a week. This will include memorizing at least one Scripture verse each week.
- Group Participation.
  -Attend the weekly group session.
  -Make up any session missed.
  -Encourage and support other group members.
  -Be accountable to the group for completion of weekly assignments.
  -Openly share in the group.
  -Pray for one another.
- Discipleship growth. Members are expected to want to grow as they progress through training.

What are some pitfalls to avoid? You will avoid problems by planning for the following situations.
- Not enough leaders for the number of members.
- Over enlistment. Let the maximum group size be known in case you are overrun with potential members.
- Agreeing to allow "observers" who want to just "sit in and listen." *Step by Step Through the New Testament* is not a spectator Bible study. Decide how you will respond to those who want the knowledge without

doing the work. Plan to encourage such persons to wait until a time when they can be a participant in the fullest sense.
- Trying to facilitate too many groups yourself. I know (from painful experience) that it is better to do a good job with one group than a poor job with several. However, you can facilitate two groups if you keep them on the same units. If you should lead two groups, schedule them at different times and on different days of the week.

Scheduling Sessions

Discipleship Training of this depth cannot be done well in less than one hour. Group sessions should last from 1 to 1½ hours. (Sessions are configured around 80 minutes or more being available. Adjust time as needed for shorter sessions). Groups may meet at the church, in homes, or other locations convenient to members. You may want to offer group studies at a variety of times and locations so more people will be able to participate. Consider these options:
- Sunday evening at church. Groups can meet prior to the evening worship service.
- Weekday evening at church. Groups can meet prior to or following the mid-week prayer service.
- Weekday morning, afternoon, or evening. Groups can meet in homes, at the church, or at work during a time convenient to participants.

Split sessions are also a possibility. You could meet on Sunday night and again after worship services on Wednesday evening. You also could choose to extend the course from 14 to 28 sessions and study only one part of a unit each week. This will call for a long-term commitment on the part of participants, but the amount of required study each week will be reduced. Choosing to extend the course will also give you additional time to read the New Testament through as you complete your study of *Step by Step Through the New Testament*. Design your schedule to meet the needs of your people.

Discipleship groups may meet anytime and anyplace that is convenient for members. The process works best when meetings are in a home. Elaborate refreshments are not recommended as they could take too much of the members' preparation and group time.

If you choose to have only one hour per week for your group sessions, the following guidelines will help you adjust the structure of the course.

Recommended Choice: two weeks per unit of study.

- Complete individual study and use the first hour's agenda for the first group session.
- Encourage individual unit review during the second week and use the second hour's agenda for the second group session. This option requires 27 weeks—an introductory session and 26 group sessions.

PREPARING TO LEAD THE STUDY

Suggestions in this section are directed to the persons who have been enlisted to serve as group leaders. Following these suggestions will help you make adequate preparation for carrying out your responsibilities and will help equip you to be an effective leader.

Your Role as a Small-Group Leader

You may be asking yourself, "Why did I agree to lead this group? I need to know more about the New Testament myself." If you sense God has led you to accept this assignment, you can trust Him to equip and enable you to accomplish the task. Your role in a small-group study is not that of a teacher. Rather, your responsibility is to facilitate the group learning process. The following guidelines are taken from *MasterBuilder: Multiplying Leaders*, and will help you facilitate the growth process with your group.

1. *Create an atmosphere of acceptance and sharing*. Room arrangement is essential to group atmosphere. Set up the room so that members are in a circle and within arm's reach of one another. Make sure the room is quiet and free of distractions.

2. *Model the attitude of a servant*. Members will take their cues from you. Ask God to help you balance the group leadership role with that of a servant to the group.

3. *Participate as a group member*. Be a part of the process. Allow God to lead the group. You often will find that once the discussion is started, the Lord will gently lead it along and make the truths relevant to the group.

4. *Involve all group members in the discussion*. "As iron sharpens iron, so one man sharpens another" (Prov. 27:17). Find ways to involve members who are hesitant to participate without embarrassing them or forcing them to be more open to the group than they are willing to be. As the members grow in their knowledge so they will grow in their ability to get into the group interaction. The truths of the Scripture will come into focus as the members test and dig into the ideas. Do not allow any member to habitually adopt the role of critic. Encourage all the members to take part.

5. Keep the group moving toward its goals. Keeping the group on track and moving toward achieving the learning goal is important. There will be times when you will have to encourage the group to get back on track or to move on in their discussion.

Prepare or Secure Additional Resources
Much of your course preparation can be completed at one time. Everything you can do before the study begins will free time later for personal and spiritual preparation. Pages 61-64 contain materials to be used during the group sessions. At the appropriate time, you will be instructed to make copies of these materials for use in the sessions. Some of the material is optional and you may or may not choose to use it. Pages 12-13 provide step-by-step directions for leading an introductory session and 13 group sessions based on members' individual study during the previous week.
1. Duplicated materials. Make copies of the following pages in this leader's guide for group members. Some are optional or may be prepared on a poster or chalkboard, so use your own judgment. You have permission to copy the following pages, but only for use with groups studying *Step by Step Through the New Testament*.
Highly Recommended:
- Unit Review Quizzes (pp. 61-64)
- Chronology of Jesus' Life Worksheet (pp. 17-18)

2. Provide markerboard or large sheets of paper and markers for use throughout the course. Keep a supply readily available.
3. Obtain a good set of Bible maps for use in the group sessions. If your church does not own a set, see whether you can borrow them from your associational office or Discipleship Training Director. They also may be ordered from LifeWay® Christian Stores (call 1-800-233-1123). Make certain you also obtain an easel on which to mount the maps.

Anticipate Difficult Questions
Expect questions you may not be able to answer. In these cases you should remind the class that you are a facilitator, not an authoritative expert. Encourage participants to join you in praying and searching the Scriptures. Together, ask God to guide you to His answer. Just as God spoke to His people in New Testament times, He will speak to you. When God answers through one or more group members, you all will know more of God through experience. Here is a vital rule for any group facilitator: you best help your members when you equip them to find their own answers.

As the group facilitator, you may want to obtain some additional study resources to aid you in your preparation. Studying the complete text before making any purchases will help ensure that you purchase those resources that will be most helpful to you.

Suggested Resources:
An Introduction to the New Testament, D. A. Carson, Douglas J. Moo, and Leon Morris, Zondervan, 1991.
Holman Bible Dictionary, Trent C. Butler, General Editor, Holman, 1991.
The Biblical Illustrator, published quarterly by LifeWay Christian Resources of the Southern Baptist Convention. Contains concise articles about cultural, historical, and biblical subjects related to quarterly Sunday School lessons. You'll find excellent material to supplement your study in *Step by Step Through the New Testament*.

CONDUCTING SESSIONS
Understand Group Session Plans' Structure
Give careful preparation to the weekly group session. This will be the time when the group will "pull it all together" and apply the truth of the Scriptures to their lives. Each group-session plan includes three parts: Before the Session, During the Session, and After the Session. Let's look more closely at each of these major divisions.

Before the Session. This section includes actions for you to complete prior to the group session. Boxes are provided for you to check as you complete each action. I have done my best to provide sessions that require a minimum of leader preparation. If you adapt the lesson plans or create activities of your own, you will need to secure any resources that are required for these activities. Most of the units will have an optional learning activity to reinforce some aspect of the content. Decide at the time you do the "Before the Session" preparation if you will do the optional identification activities for that particular unit.

During the Session. This section provides questions and learning activities for use in conducting a group session. The activities follow a similar pattern each week. The first part reviews the content of the unit members studied during the previous week. The second part focuses on discussion and assimilation of the biblical content.

Each session concludes with a prayer time, followed by a preview of the next unit. If you choose to assign the optional activity for the next session, you will make the assignment during the conclusion.

Here is what a session schedule should look like.

Part 1 (30-45 minutes)
1. Group Time
   This time allows members to relax and share what they have been experiencing.
2. Review Time
   During this segment members have a unit review quiz which calls for them to review or recall key people, places, ideas, dates, and Scripture passages from the unit content they studied during the previous week. Answers to the review quiz for each week are given in the training plan for that week.

Break (5 minutes)

Part 2 (30-45 minutes)
3. Bible Study and Group Discussion
   Discussion, check-up, and affective learning activities will help members understand and apply the session content.
4. Preview Next Week's Assignment
   Content and activities for the following week will be introduced, interest will be generated for the coming unit, and prayer will be offered.

After the Session. This section guides you in evaluating the group session, your performance as a leader, and the needs of group members. It is intended to help you constantly improve your abilities to guide the group members in their learning and spiritual growth. Each week you are encouraged to pray for your group members and identify one or more who may need a personal contact from you. I hope you will not neglect this aspect of your ministry. Your primary assignment in this study is to help people grow in Christ, not just teach knowledge. Remember, disciple making is investing your life in others!

Coping with Problems
1. Members who are absent. Ask members to tell you before the session if they will be absent. If they do not, contact them as soon as possible after the session. Arrange to meet them for a make-up session. Do not let them get two or three weeks behind, or they probably will drop out.

2. Members who do not complete their homework. Expect homework assignments to be completed using an honor system. You might want to ask persons who have not completed assignments related to the topic under discussion not to ask questions during that portion of the session. Meet privately with individuals who are struggling to encourage them to remain current. Help them resolve problems they may be experiencing. They cannot receive the benefit of *Step by Step Through the New Testament* if they do not do their study. If the problem persists, suggest that perhaps this is not the right time for them to complete the course, and that they withdraw until a later time. This sounds harsh. However, if they do not do their work, they will hurt the spirit and motivation of the entire group.

3. Members who want to drop out. Many times members have not studied seriously for years and are out of the habit. Do what you can to encourage them to stick with the course and manage their time better. If they must drop out, do not make them feel guilty. Encourage them to look for an opportunity to complete the course at a later date.

4. Members who do not agree with the content. Some debate in the group is good. The Scriptures always should be the final source of authority. If debate becomes counter productive, you may just say, "Why don't you and I get together and discuss this later? Our time is limited here and others also want to ask questions." This will defuse a possible disagreement and allow you to complete the group session.

5. Members who dominate the group. As the leader, make sure every person gets an opportunity to share. You may discourage dominating members by calling on other persons, asking that someone who has not spoken yet answer the next question, focusing your attention on someone else, and so forth. Some groups may take care of the problem themselves by their reactions to the dominating person. If those methods do not work, talk privately with the person who is dominating. Ask that person's help in getting everyone to participate in the discussion. As a last resort, state the problem candidly and ask for his/her cooperation.

6. Not enough time in the session. Start and stop on time. Keep the group moving toward ending the session on schedule. Be punctual so members can pick up children and meet other engagements. If insufficient time is a persistent problem, the group may need to negotiate a longer session time if you are using less than 1½ hours.

7. Refreshments can be a problem. Keep refreshments simple. Do not allow persons to try to outdo one another. Make coffee and soft drinks available. Do not let the brief break in the middle of the session get out of hand. It is better to fellowship before or after the session.

8. Provisions for child care. If the group meets at the church during the Discipleship Training time, training should be provided for children and youth using recommended Discipleship Training resources. However, you may need to get someone to come early if you have 1½-hour sessions. If you meet at another time, members may pay for a baby sitter. Another church member may volunteer to care for the children this quarter, in turn for your getting someone to take care of his or her children next quarter. Sometimes the church will provide child care.

Set and Collect Fees
Group members should be expected to pay for the cost of materials. Your church may want to share the cost, but members should share some part of the expense. (I have found in years of working with LIFE courses, that not one person has ever lost a book he/she paid for.) Announce the fee at the time you enlist participants so they will not be embarrassed or surprised at the introductory session. You may want to provide some type scholarship for those who would need assistance.

STAYING ON TRACK
Keep Records
Work with the Discipleship Training director or general secretary to determine the best way of keeping enrollment and attendance records. Participation in a LIFE course such as *Step by Step Through the New Testament* counts toward Discipleship Training participation regardless of the time of week it is offered. Report your weekly attendance to the Discipleship Training director or secretary. If your church does not have an ongoing Discipleship Training program, you can still count participation in *Step by Step Through the New Testament* on the Discipleship Training section of the Annual Church Profile.

The church study course is another reason to record participation. Persons who complete the individual study of *Step by Step Through the New Testament* and attend the group sessions qualify for the course diploma. These diplomas recognize the participants' significant work.

Evaluate the Group Sessions[1]
Use the following questions to evaluate each group session. Make notes to jog your memory the next time you lead a group through this study.
1. Do you believe members achieved the session learning goals? Why or why not?
2. Did you dominate the discussion, or did you serve as a facilitator to involve members in the discussion?
3. Was everyone involved in learning activities? Do not force shy members, but encourage all to participate.
4. Did you show a genuine interest in each member of the group? What could have been done to create more interest and participation?
5. Did the session move smoothly and orderly?
6. What did you learn from the session that you should remember and use as you plan for the next session?
7. Do you need to make any personal contacts to encourage members of the group?

A Personal Word
While working on this leader guide, I was reminded of how like the early Christians we are. The Holy Spirit led these early Christians to witness for Jesus in the same way He leads us today. We are not so different from those who lived before us. We simply live at a different time in history. A distinct pattern emerges—those who know Jesus carry the message of salvation to those who do not. Those who are walking with Jesus live as an example for those who have not met Him. The body of Christ encourages and disciples one another under Christ's leadership while ministering in the daily marketplace.

As you use this leader guide to facilitate others through *Step by Step Through the New Testament,* I pray you will be caught up in the excitement of walking daily with the Lord. You will see session goals at the beginning of each session, but the ultimate purpose of the leader guide can be stated in the words of the apostle Paul, "We proclaim him, admonishing and teaching everyone with all wisdom, so that we may present everyone perfect in Christ" (Col. 1:28). As you disciple those God entrusts to you, I pray that you, like Paul, will "Labor, struggling with all his energy, which so powerfully works in (you) me" (Col. 1:29).

---
[1]Adapted from Arthur H. Criscoe, Leonard Sanderson, *DecisionTime:Commitment Counseling* (Nashville: Baptist Sunday School Board, 1989), 266.

Introducing Step by Step Through the New Testament

SESSION GOALS

In this session members will:

1. Be introduced to the course *Step by Step Through the New Testament*.

2. Understand the requirements of the course.

3. Make a commitment to complete this study of the New Testament.

Before the Session

❑ 1. Study carefully the course Administrative Guide (pp. 5-11) and review the session goals above.

❑ 2. Pray for God's guidance as you prepare for this group session. Pray for those who will be present, specifically for those who may still be hesitant about coming.

❑ 3. Read through "During the Session." Decide on the amount of time to allow for each segment of the session. Write in the margin of your Leader Guide the time you want each segment to begin.

❑ 4. Gather copies of *Step by Step Through the New Testament* member book for each person coming to the introductory meeting.

During the Session

OPENING ACTIVITIES (20 MINUTES)

1. Welcome everyone and begin with prayer. If the participants do not know each other, make sure each participant has a name tag.

2. Make introductions. Spend a few minutes becoming acquainted with group members.

3. Give each person a three-by-five card or small piece of paper. Have him/her record on the paper:
   - a. Name.
   - b. Number of siblings in his/her childhood home.
   - c. Age at which he/she learned to ride a bicycle.
   - d. One fact about him/her most people would not know unless told.

4. When they are finished have them pass the cards in to you. Read the information on each card and have members try to guess who the card is about. If no one can guess, have the person identify himself.

Explain How the Course Works

1. Individual Study. Emphasize the importance of doing the work each day and week. Explain that members will want to discipline themselves to spend time daily in meeting God through the pages of *Step by Step Through the New Testament* and through the pages of the New Testament itself. Encourage them to begin now with a commitment to do each day's work as it comes. Tell them accountability for the assignments is built into the group process.

2. Group Sessions. Tell them attendance at the group sessions is part of the course requirements. The members will want to make certain they have the time to attend the group sessions before signing up for this course. Missed sessions will need to be made up with you in a private session.

Introduce *Step by Step Through the New Testament*
Say, Our study of the New Testament in *Step by Step Through the New Testament* will be an exciting encounter with God as we examine His work through the life and ministry of Jesus and as we examine the beginning of the church. The purpose of the course will be for you to experience God anew through the New Testament. Ask members, *What do you want most to gain from this study of the New Testament?* Allow members time to respond.

Hand Out Materials—10 Minutes

1. Give each member a copy of the member's book for the course. Instruct them to look at the table of contents and select units they think will be of particular interest to them.

2. Ask several members to share the units they selected and why.

CONCLUSION—10 MINUTES

1. Preview next week's materials. Note that the next session is entitled "God and the New Covenant." The session content will be an introduction to the people and environment of Palestine at the time the New Testament was written.

2. Make assignments for the next session. The assigned members will want to be prepared to give brief (no more than two minutes) reports on the subject. These assignments should mention the significant persons, events, and dates related to the report. The subjects to be assigned are:
   - Events related to the rise of Rome
   - Summary of events in the section "The Jewish State"
   - Summary of events in the section "Outside the Jewish State"
   - Report on the section entitled "The Social World"
   - Report on the section "Sects of Judaism"

3. Remind the group to do their work daily and that each one will have an opportunity to participate in the group sessions during the follow-up of the reports given.

4. Remind members of the group session's time and place.

5. As you pray together, pray specifically for each member to reorder his or her time as necessary to complete this study of the New Testament.

After the Session

1. Carefully evaluate the effectiveness of the session.
   - Do you believe members achieved the session learning goals?
   - Did you dominate the discussion, or did you as a facilitator involve members in the discussion?
   - Were all members involved in learning activities?
   - Did you show a genuine interest in each member of the group? What could have been done to create more interest and participation?
   - Did the session move smoothly and in an orderly fashion?

2. What did you learn from the session that you should remember and use as you plan for the next session?

3. Do you need to make any personal contacts to encourage members of the group?

4. Save materials you have developed for use in future groups of *Step by Step Through the New Testament*.

5. Immediately begin your preparation for next week's group session.

6. Pray for the group. This week pray for members' ability to discern God's will as He reveals Himself, His purposes, and His ways to them in the pages of the New Testament.

GROUP SESSION 1

God and the New Covenant

SESSION GOALS

 At the conclusion of this session members will be able to:

1. Understand the significant personalities, religions, and cultural factors surrounding the New Testament.

2. Identify the sects of first-century Judaism.

3. Define the concept of the canon of the New Testament.

4. List three criteria for a writing being accepted as part of the canon.

5. State three principles of interpretation.

Before the Session

❑ 1. Study carefully unit 1 and complete all learning activities. Review the group session goals above.
❑ 2. Pray for God's guidance as you prepare for this group session. Pray specifically for each member.
❑ 3. Read through "During the Session." You may not have time in the session to cover all the questions in your Leader Guide. Ask God to guide you to the questions He wants discussed with the group. Decide on the amount of time to allow for each segment of the Bible study. Write in the margin of your Leader Guide the time you want each segment to begin.
❑ 4. Gather the following materials:
 • Copies of the unit review quiz to pass out to group members.
 • A set of maps to use in the Bible study segment each week.
 • Note paper for members.

❑ 5. Extra Preparation:
 • Contact your host if you're meeting in a home. Make certain he or she knows when to expect the group and how many plan to come.
 • Make a copy of the Chronology of Jesus' Life Worksheet for each member.

During the Session

Part I
OPENING ACTIVITIES—20 MINUTES

1. Welcome members and begin with prayer. (5 mins.)

2. Distribute and have members complete the unit review quiz. When they have finished, lead a discussion of their answers. (10 Minutes) Quiz Answers: 1-A, 2-H, 3-G, 4-B, 5-I, 6-F, 7-C, 8-J, 9-E, 10-D.

Part II
BIBLE STUDY AND GROUP DISCUSSION—50 MINUTES

God and the New Covenant
Begin with the person to your right and have the group recall the six goals of *Step by Step Through the New Testament*. (These are listed as 6 features of New Testament study on p. 5.) Your goals would be to:
1. Examine the nature of the New Testament.
2. Study the world of the New Testament.
3. Investigate the text of the New Testament.
4. Identify the authors of the New Testament.
5. Explore the contents of the New Testament.
6. Practice principles of interpretation of the New Testament.

Have a member explain in a couple of sentences the difference between the Old and New Testaments.

Have the group turn to the activity in day 1, "Reasons for Studying the New Testament." Ask several to state at least one reason they want to study the New Testament.

The Roman Empire
Have the assigned member give his summary of the rise of the Roman Empire.

Turn in your member book to the margin heading "Roman Rulers During the New Testament Period." Call out the names of the Roman rulers during the New Testament period. As you do, ask the group to recall at least one significant fact about each.

Ask the group to recall the two types of Provinces in the Roman Empire. (1 - Senatorial Provinces—these were peaceful and were under the Roman Senate. They were presided over by an officer known as a pro-consul. 2- Imperial Provinces—these were more turbulent and were ruled by an imperial appointee called a procurator).

Ask the group to recall the meaning of the term "Pax Romana" (Roman Peace). Ask, What was the historical significance of this for the early church? (It allowed for rapid and unhindered expansion of the church.)

The Jewish State
Call for the report on the Jewish State. Choose from the following questions to bring out content not covered in the report.
- Which Persian king released the Jews from captivity? (Cyrus, in 538 B.C.)
- How many Jews returned to Palestine? (42,000)
- Who led the first group of returning Jews? (Sheshbazzar)
- Who came 80 years later with a second delegation of Jews? (Ezra)
- Who came 13 years after Ezra and mobilized the people to complete the task of building the wall of Jerusalem? (Nehemiah)

Outside the Jewish State
Call for the report on events outside the Jewish State. Choose from the following questions to bring out content not covered in the report.
- Who brought Greek culture to Palestine? (Alexander the Great)
- Who was Ptolomy and his followers (often called Ptolomies)? (Followers of the General who gained control of Egypt and Palestine from 320-198 B.C.)
- Who were the Seleucids? (Rulers from Syria who gained control of Palestine from 198-168 B.C.)
- Which Seleucid ruler set up a statue of Zeus in the Jewish temple? (Antiochus Epiphanes)
- What Jewish leader led the revolt of 167 B.C.? (Mattathias)
- Which Maccabean leader eventually expelled the Syrians from Palestine in 142 B.C. (Simon)
- Who were the Hasmoneans? (Politically-minded descendants of the Maccabeans)
- Who were the Hasidim? (Devout Jews who opposed the political aims of the Hasmoneans)
- What later group was descended from the Hasmonean rulers? (the Sadducees)
- What group later descended from the Hasidim (devout Jews)? (the Pharisees)

Jewish Society
Call for the report on "The Social World." Use the following questions to bring out additional content.
- How many Jews lived in the Roman Empire during New Testament times? (4,000,000)
- How many Jews lived in Palestine? (700,000)
- What was the common language? (Aramic)
- What was the religious language? (Hebrew)
- What percentage of the population were slaves in the Roman Empire?
- In the pagan world what types of professions were open to slaves? (Physicians, teachers, skilled craftsmen, almost all trades)
- What were some of the problems that resulted from slavery? (p. 13)

The Religious World
Have the group recall the names of the religious groups prevalent in the first century. You may refer them to day 3, The Religious World, for this information.

Ask, Why was refusal to engage in Emperor worship regarded as treason? (Because the emperor was considered as a god)

Refer the group to the statement on page 14, "Emperor worship made support of the state a religious duty, and the refusal of Christians to practice it exposed them to persecution." Note that this dilemma is in the background of much of the New Testament period.

Ask, What were characteristics of the mystery religions? (Eastern origin, offered more personal contact with deity, promised immortality, outlet for emotional experiences) Ask, What were some other religious groups in the first century? (Gnostics, Epicureans, Stoics, Skeptics)

The Jewish World
Ask the group to recall the three basic characteristics of the first-century Judaism. (Emphasized monotheism, provided an ethical emphasis in its religious life, and based on the sacred Scriptures)

Ask, What did first-century Jews expect in a Messiah? (Political-military ruler)

How did Jesus differ from their expectations?

Have members recall the three purposes of the Jewish Synagogues. (A place for: study and teaching of the law, instruction of children, and social contact.)

Call for the report on the Sects of Judaism. If it is not covered in the report, be sure the group understands the basic differences between the Pharisees, Sadducees, and Essenes. You may refer them to page 18 for this information.

The Text and Canon of the New Testament
Ask, What is your response to knowing that early Christians possessed only the Old Testament for Scriptures? (It reminds us the Old Testament is Scripture too).

Discuss the concept of *canon* using these questions:
- What was the original meaning of the term *canon*?
- How did the term come to be used of the New Testament Scriptures?

Discuss the criteria for the books of the canon using the following question.
- What criteria did the churches use in determining the books of the canon? (Authored by an apostle or associate of an apostle, teachings consistent with apostolic doctrine, morally edifying and accepted by the church).

Have the group recall the principles of interpretation.
 a. Interpret the Bible literally.
 b. Interpret Scripture in light of its setting.
 c. Accept the limits of God's revelation.
 d. Distinguish between interpretation and application.
 e. Interpret difficult texts with help from clearer texts.

Refer the members to the activity at the end of day 5 in which they were to apply the principles of interpretation. Have them share which principles they matched with the Scripture texts in the activity. As time permits, lead members in a discussion of the principles or interpretation using the author's illustrations. You want them to discuss and understand the five principles of interpretation.

CONCLUSION—10 MINUTES

1. Use the introduction you prepared to preview next week's materials. Ask members to look at the unit overview appearing at the beginning of unit 2. Next week they will be studying, "Introduction to the Gospels." Distribute copies of the Chronology of Jesus' Life Worksheet at this time. Tell the members this worksheet will be used to help them gain an overview of Jesus' life and ministry, and will help them as they study this week.
2. Remind members of the importance of doing the work. Encourage them to make time daily to work in their books. They want to develop the practice of spending time with God daily.

After the Session

1. Carefully evaluate the effectiveness of the session. Use the questions that appear on page 11 in the course administrative plan to guide your evaluation.
2. Save any materials you have developed for use in future groups of *Step by Step Through the New Testament*.
3. Immediately begin your preparations for next week's session.
4. Pray for each member by name this week. They will be studying the kingdom of God and Jesus' reign over their lives. Pray for each participant to be completely secure in his/her salvation and growing in his/her relationship to Christ.

A Chronology of Events, Miracles, and Parables in Jesus' Life and Ministry

Parables appear in bold type and *miracles in italicized type*. Other events and references appear in standard type.

	Matthew	Mark	Luke	John
<u>The Birth and Early life of Jesus</u>				
Birth of Jesus:	1:18-25:		2:1-7	
Shepherds Visit:			2:8-20	
Presentation in Temple:			2:21-40	
Visit of the Wise Men:	2:1-12			
Escape to Egypt:	2:13-15			
Return to Palestine:	2:19-23			
Boyhood Visit to Temple:			2:41-52	
<u>The Beginning of Jesus' Ministry</u>				
Jesus Baptized:	3:13-17;	1:9-11;	3:21-23;	1:29-34
Jesus Tempted by Satan:	4:1-11;	1:12-13;	4:1-13	
<u>Jesus' Galilean Ministry</u>				
Water Turned to Wine:				2:1-11
Healing; Man with an Unclean Spirit:		1:23-26;	4:33-35	
Healing; Official's Son:				4:46-54
Calling of the First Disciples:	4:18-22;	1:16-20;	5:1-11;	1:35-52
Healings:	4:23-24;	1:32-34		
A Miraculous Catch of Fish:			5:4-11	
The Sermon on the Mount:	5:1—7:29;		6:20-49	
Lamp Under a Bowl:	5:14-16;	4:21-22;	8:16; 11:33	
Builders:	7:24-27;		6:46-49	
Healing of a Leper:	8:1-4;	1:40-42;	5:12-13	
Healing of the Centurian's Servant:	8:5-13		7:1-10	
Healing of Peter's Mother-in-law:	8:14-15;	1:29-31;	4:38-39	
Healing of a Blind Man:				9:1-12
Raising of a Widow's Son:			7:11-15	
Calming of the Storm at Sea:	8:23-27;	4:35-42;	8:22-25	
Healing of the Wild Men of Gadara:	8:28-34;	5:1-15;	8:26-35	
Healing of a Paralytic:	9:1-7;	2:1-12;	5:18-25	
Call of Matthew:	9:9-13;	2:13-17;	5:27-32	
New Cloth on Old Coat:	9:16;	2:21;	5:36	
New Wine in Old Skins:	9:17;	2:22;	5:37-38	
Choosing of the Twelve:	10:1-4;	3:13-19;	6:12-16	
Growing Seed:		4:26-29		
Moneylender:			7:41-43	
Healing of a Deaf, Speechless Man:		7:31-37		
Healing of a Blind Man at Bethsaida:		8:22-26		
Raising of Jairus' Daughter:	9:18-19,23-25;	5:22-24, 35-43;	8:40-42,49-56	
Healing of a Woman with a Hemorrhage:	9:20-22;	5:25-34;	8:43-48	
Healing of Two Blind Men:	9:27-31			
Lame Man at Bethesda:				5:1-9
Healing of a Demon-possessed Man:	8:32-33			
Healing of a Man with a Shriveled Hand:	12:10-13;	3:1-5;	6:6-10	
Sower and Soils:	13:3-8, 18-23;	4:3-8, 14-20;	8:5-8, 11-15	
Weeds and Wheat:	13:24-30, 36-43			
Mustard Seed:	13:31-32;	4:30-32;	13:18-10	
Yeast:	13:33;		13:20-21	
Hidden Treasure:	13:44			
Valuable Pearl:	13:45-56			
Net:	13:47, 50			
Owner of a House:	13:52			
Feeding of 5,000 People:	13:13-21;	6:32-44;	9:10-17;	6:1-13
Walking on the Sea:	14:22-25;	6:47-51;		6:16-21
Healing; Syrophoenician's Daughter:	15:21-28;	7:24-30		
Feeding of 4,000 People:	15:32-38;	8:1-10		
Peter's Confession:	16:13-20;	8:27-29;	9:18-20	
The Transfiguration:	17:1-8;	9:2-8;	9:28-36	
Healing of a Boy with Seizures:	17:14-18;	9:14-29;	9:37-43	
Lost Sheep:	18:12-14;		15:4-7	
Unmerciful Servant:	18:23-34			

	Matthew	Mark	Luke	John
Jesus' Final Journey to Jerusalem				
Vineyard Workers:	20:1-16			
Good Samaritan:			10:30-37	
Friends in Need:			11:5-8	
Rich Fool:			12:16-21	
Unfruitful Fig Tree:			13:6-9	
Healing of an Infirm Woman:			13:11-13	
Healing of a Man with Dropsy:			14:1-4	
Low Seat at Feast:			14:7-14	
Great Banquet:			14:16-24	
Cost of Discipleship:			14:28-33	
Lost Coin:			15:8-10	
Prodigal Son:			15:11-32	
Shrewd Manager:			16:1-8	
Rich Man and Lazarus:			16:19-31	
Master and Servant:			17:7-10	
Healing of Ten Lepers:			17:11-19	
Persistent Widow:			18:2-8	
Pharisee and Tax Collector:			18:10-14	
Healing of Two Blind Men at Jericho:	20:30-34			
Healing of Blind Bartimaeus:		10:46-52		
Raising of Lazarus:				11:38-44
Jesus' Final Week, Crucifixion and Burial				
SUNDAY				
The Triumphal Entry:	21:1-11;	11:1-10;	19:29-44;	12:12-19
MONDAY				
Jesus Cleanses the Temple:	21:12-13;	11:15-18		
Jesus Curses the Fig Tree:	21:18-19;	11:12-14		
TUESDAY				
Jesus Teaches in the Temple:	21:23-27;	11:27-33;	20:1-8	
Two Sons:	21:28-32			
Tenants:	21:33-44;	12:1-11	20:1-8	
Wedding Banquet:	22:2-14			
Jesus Teaches the Disciples:	24:1—25:46			
Fig Tree:	24:32-35;	13:28-29;	21:29-31	
Faithful and Wise Servant:	24:45-51:		12:42-48	
Ten Virgins:	24:1-13			
Talents:	24:14-30;		19:12-27	
Sheep and Goats:	24:31-46			
Watchful Servants:		13:35-37	12:35-40	
WEDNESDAY				
The Jews Plot Against Jesus:	26:2-5, 14-15;	14:1-2, 10-11;	22:1-6	
THURSDAY				
The Lord's Supper:	26:17-30;	14:12-25;	22:7-20;	13:1-38
Gethsemane:	26:36-46;	14:32-42:	22:40-46	
Arrest and Trial:	26:47—27:31;	14:43—15:20;	22:47—23:25;	18:1—19:16
Healing of Malchus' Ear:		22:50-51;	18:3-11	
FRIDAY				
Crucifixion, Death, and Burial:	27:32-66;	15:21-47;	23:26-56;	19:16-42
The Resurrection and Post Resurrection Narratives				
The Resurrection:	28;	16;	24;	20
A Second Miraculous Catch of Fish:				21:1-14
The Reinstatement of Simon Peter:				21:1-23
The Great Commission:	28:18-20			

You have permission to reproduce this form for use with your LIFE course small group.

GROUP SESSION 2

Introduction to the Gospels

SESSION GOALS

 At the conclusion of this session members will:

1. Explain why the gospels are the authentic accounts of Jesus' life and ministry.

2. Understand the relative size and features of the land of Palestine.

3. State reasons for assurance of their salvation.

4. Understand the events surrounding the birth, life, and ministry of Jesus.

Before the Session

❏ 1. Study carefully unit 2 and complete all learning activities. Review the group session goals above.
❏ 2. Pray for God's guidance as you prepare for this group session. Pray specifically for each member of your group.
❏ 3. Read through "During the Session." You may not have time in the session to cover all the questions in your Leader Guide. Ask God to guide you to the questions He wants discussed with the group. Decide on the amount of time to allow for each segment of the Bible study. Write in the margin of your Leader Guide the time you want each segment to begin.
❏ 4. Gather copies of the unit review quiz to pass out to group members.
❏ 5. Extra Preparation:
 • Palestine is a land of approximately 10,000 square miles. Using a state map or road atlas, find the size of your state in relation to Palestine. For example, the state of Tennessee (in which LifeWay Christian Resources is located) consists of approximately 42,000 square miles. Divided by the number 10,000, we determine that Tennessee is 4.2 times bigger than the land of Palestine. After discovering the size of your state in relation to Palestine, be prepared to share this in the group session. This will help group members understand more of the land in which God revealed Himself most fully to us.
 • Prepare two slips of paper to be used in subgroup discussion. Subgroup number one will discuss the question, What is the basis of assurance of our salvation? Subgroup number two will discuss the question, What are some reasons why people doubt their salvation?
 • Provide for refreshments if they are being served during the break.
 • Prepare a two-minute introduction to the next unit to be given in the conclusion of this unit.

During the Session

Part I
OPENING ACTIVITIES—20 MINUTES

1. Welcome members and begin with prayer. (5 mins.)

2. Distribute and have members complete the unit review quiz. When they have finished, lead a discussion of their answers. (10 mins.) Quiz Answers: 1-B, 2-D, 3-F, 4-H, 5-J, 6-A, 7-C, 8-E, 9-G, 10-I.

Part II
BIBLE STUDY AND GROUP DISCUSSION—50 MINUTES

Reliable Witnesses: The Four Gospels
Ask the group to recall sources other than the Gospels that speak of Jesus. (The Jewish historian Josephus, and the Roman writer Tacitus)

Ask, What are two questionable sources that supposedly speak to the life of Jesus? (The *Gospel of Thomas* and the so-called *Infancy Gospels*)

Ask, Why are the four Gospels of the canon our reliable account of Jesus life and ministry? (Possible Answers: They present a true picture of the Divine Redeemer. Their descriptions are spiritually moving and fully reliable. The answers could also include the criteria for the canon studied in unit 1.)

Have a member locate on a map of Palestine the places Jesus visited and ministered. (You may refer to the section on day 1, "The Geography of Jesus' Life," for a list of the places.

The Geography of Palestine

Have another member use the map and give a brief description of the geography of Palestine. After the member has finished, use the following questions as needed to cover the content:
- What is the size of Palestine in square miles?
- How far is it from
  - Caesarea to Gaza (80 Miles)
  - Mt. Lebanon, to Dead Sea (175 Miles)
  - Mediterranean to Sea of Galilee (28 Miles)
  - Mediterranean to the Dead Sea (54 Miles)
- What are the major features of the area? (Coastal Plains, Hill Country, Jordan Valley, Jordan River, Sea of Galilee, Dead Sea, Eastern Plateau (which is known as the Decapolis)
- How large is the Sea of Galilee? (Thirteen miles long by eight miles wide)
- What were the three provinces existing in Palestine in the first century? (Galilee, Samaria, and Judea)

Ask, What were the predominate population groups located in each area? (Gentiles in Galilee, Samaritans in Samaria, and Jews in Judea)

Jesus: His Teaching and Ministry

Refer the group to Mark 8:1-3. Ask, What most impressed you about Jesus' teaching in this passage? After several have shared, lead the group in a brief prayer for them to hear Jesus anew as they study His life and ministry.

Have the group recall characteristics of Jesus' teaching (used sharp contrasts and strong statements, was authoritative, used parables, used picturesque speech, used exaggeration (hyperbole), sometimes used argument, used questions and answers, used object lessons)

Read the author's statement appearing on page 31: "Jesus never organized His teachings into a system. He organized the teaching around His own person." After you read the statement, ask the group to discuss this statement: "Spiritual truth is not a concept to be thought about, debated, or discussed. Truth is a Person."[1]

God's Kingdom and Our Salvation

Use these questions to discuss the kingdom of God.
- What is the kingdom of God? (the reign of God over His people)
- How do the Jews enter into God's kingdom? (they enter it like everyone else)
- What is the relationship between the church and the Kingdom? (The church is not identical with the kingdom, but the ministry of the church does help spread the Kingdom.)
- How does one enter the Kingdom? (by repentance and faith)
- What is included in repentance? (change of mind about Jesus and sin, and a change of behavior to be obedient to Jesus)
- What is included in faith? (trust in Jesus Christ for deliverance from sin, and allowing Him control of our lives)

Activity. Be sensitive to the members during the discussion of salvation. Make a mental note of members who are uncomfortable. A discreet visit could help someone be sure that he has a valid personal relationship with Christ that is real and growing. Allow 15 minutes on this activity.

Divide the group into two subgroups. Ask one to discuss, "What is the basis of assurance of our salvation?" (Answers may vary: Some possible answers are our personal experience with Christ, promise of God's Word, power of God to keep those who are His)

---

[1]Henry T. Blackaby and Claude V. King, *Experiencing God: Knowing and Doing the Will of God* (Nashville: LifeWay Press, 1990), 87.

Ask the other group to discuss, "What are some reasons people doubt their salvation?" (Answers may vary. Some possible answers are they have not met Christ, they have sin in their life, they need to grow in their knowledge and walk with the Lord each day.) Allow five minutes for discussion.

Call the groups back to the large group. Each subgroup will have five minutes to report.

An Overview of Jesus' Ministry
Ask, Why is dating the time of Jesus birth, ministry, death and resurrection important? (Answers may vary. Possible answers are that dating Jesus reminds us our Savior lived in human history as a real person. He died a real death on a Roman cross and was actually raised from death to be seen by His disciples after His resurrection.) Refer the group to the "Comparison of the Four Gospels" chart on page 25 in their books. Tell the group, We will discuss the specific time periods of Jesus' life and ministry in succeeding units. For now we want to gain an overview of the events of His life.

Year One: Obscurity
1. What is the term used to refer to the first year of Jesus' ministry? (Obscurity)
2. Name teachers or other Christian leaders you know of who spent a long time in obscurity before God used them publicly.
3. Can you think of a little recognized member of our church who performs valuable service for the Lord?

Year Two: Popularity
1. What term refers to Jesus' second year of ministry? (Popularity)
2. Where was Jesus' home base during His first year of ministry? (Galilee)
3. Where was Jesus' home base during His second year of ministry? (Capernaum)
4. Why did the five thousand want to make Jesus a king?

Year Three: Rejection
1. Why did Jesus reject their offer?
2. Why did Jesus' popularity begin to decline?
3. What does the rejection of Jesus by the multitudes have to say to us?
4. What two activities characterized the third year of Jesus' ministry? (traveled a lot into the Gentile areas, spent more time with his disciples)

Have the group open their Bibles to Matthew 16:13-17. Remind them that this is Simon's confession at Caesarea.
- Ask, Why was Simon Peter's confession so important? (Because God had revealed the truth about Jesus to him, and the disciples had stayed in close relationship with their master)
- What does this have to say to us?

Jesus' Final Week
Have the group recall the events of Jesus' final week by asking them, What happened on Monday, Tuesday, and so on, until you cover the week. (You may refer them to the activity at the beginning of day 5.)

Ask, What are three biblical evidences that Jesus actually died on the cross? (He was buried by friends, Roman soldiers guarded His tomb, and the women came to care for His body.)

Ask, What are some evidences of the resurrection? (Jesus appeared to Peter, James, the other apostles, and to over five hundred of His followers; the birth of the church; changed lives and the dynamic proclamation of the disciples.)

CONCLUSION—10 MINUTES

1. Using the two-minute summary you prepared, preview next week's materials. Ask members to look at the unit overview appearing at the beginning of unit 3.
2. Remind members of the importance of doing the work. Encourage them to make time daily to work in their member books. They want to develop the practice of spending time with God daily.

After the Session

1. Carefully evaluate the effectiveness of the session. Use the questions that appear on page 11 in the course administrative plan to guide your evaluation.
2. Pray for the group. This week pray for all members to sense the reality of the person and power of Christ as they begin study in the Gospels.

GROUP SESSION 3 — The Gospel of Matthew

SESSION GOALS

 At the conclusion of this session members will:

1. Explain the uniqueness of the Gospel of Matthew.

2. State truths seen in the example of Joseph.

3. Discuss principles of reconciliation and forgiveness.

4. Explain the relationship between love and obedience.

Before the Session

❑ 1. Study carefully unit 3 and complete all learning activities. Review the group session goals.

❑ 2. Pray for God's guidance as you prepare for this group session. Pray specifically for each member of your group.

❑ 3. Read through "During the Session." You may not have time in the session to cover all the questions in your Leader Guide. Ask God to guide you to the questions He wants discussed with the group. Decide on the amount of time to allow for each segment of the Bible study. Write in the margin of your Leader Guide the time you want each segment to begin.

❑ 4. Gather copies of the unit review quiz to pass out to group members.

❑ 5. Provide for refreshments if they are being served during the break.

During the Session

PART I
OPENING ACTIVITIES—20 MINUTES

1. Welcome members and begin with prayer. (5 mins.)

2. Distribute and have members complete the unit review quiz. When they have finished, lead a discussion of their answers. (10 mins.) Quiz Answers: 1-C, 2-B, 3-D, 4-E, 5-A.

Part II
BIBLE STUDY AND GROUP DISCUSSION—50 MINUTES

The Gospel of Matthew
Have the group recall the importance of the Gospel of Matthew (most quoted, most systematic, clearly arranged, and records discourses of Jesus that other gospels do not).

Ask the group to recall the special characteristics of Matthew's Gospel. (highlights the teachings of Jesus, on Jesus' miracles, only Gospel to use the word church, written in a Jewish style, frequent use of the Old Testament, strong emphasis on ethics and the designation of God as "Father in Heaven")

Ask the group to state reasons this Gospel is attributed to the apostle Matthew. (early church overwhelmingly accepted his authorship, well-organized structure indicates the orderly mind of an accountant, and it is the only Gospel recording the story of Jesus paying the Temple tax)

Ask a member to recall the most probable date of this gospel. (A.D. 60-70)

Ask, Why are Matthew, Mark, and Luke referred to as the "Synoptic Gospels"? (They look at Christ in a similar manner, *synoptic* meaning *same as*.)

Ask, What was Matthew's purpose in recording the miracles of Jesus? (to remind the disciples of the power available to them as they went out to witness in Jesus' name)

Read the author's statement appearing on page 45: "That same power is available for us today as we serve Him." Then ask the following questions:
- Do you agree or disagree with the author's statement? Have a member read 2 Timothy 1:7 and state God has given us a spirit of power.
- Is this referring to the Holy Spirit?

Have a member read Acts 1:8 and then ask:
- Does God's Spirit give us the power we need to witness for Him?
- If we are not experiencing the power of God in our lives, what is the source of the problem?

Ask the group why Jews would be interested in Jesus' genealogy through Joseph since Jesus was not really Joseph's son? (It showed the legal line of descent as reckoned through the father's lineage.)

Jesus' Birth and Early Years
(Related cross references to the scriptural accounts of Jesus' birth and early years are:
- The birth of Jesus - Matthew 1:18-25; Luke 2:1-7;
- The Shepherds Visit - Luke 2:8-20;
- The Presentation of Jesus in the Temple - Luke 2:21-40;
- The visit of the Magi - Matthew 2:1-12;
- The escape to Egypt - Matthew 2:1-12;
- The return to Palestine - Matthew 2:19-23;
- The childhood visit to the Temple - Luke 2:41-52.

The Virgin Birth (Matt. 1:18-25)
Using a map of Palestine, have a member point out the places related to Jesus' birth.

Have a member recall the basic facts of the birth account.

Ask the group the following questions as they discuss the birth account of Jesus:
- What was the nature of the crisis facing Joseph as he considered his forthcoming marriage to Mary? (her unexpected pregnancy, his and her reputation, the identity of the father of the child, his legal and religious obligations)
- How did God intervene in the situation from Joseph's perspective? (God sent His messenger to Joseph to reveal His will, and to reorient Joseph's perspective on a difficult set of circumstances)
- How was the crisis redefined when the angel of God spoke to him? (It both complicated and simplified the nature of Joseph's response. He was then confronted with a choice between doing what his natural inclinations might dictate or doing what God wanted him to do.)
- How did Joseph respond? (obediently)
- What lessons does Joseph's example hold for us?

Ask the group to discuss this statement: "What you do in response to God's revelation … reveals what you believe about God."[1]

Lead the group to understand that our faith (belief) is expressed by what we do, not simply by what we say.

Lead the group in a prayer to be obedient to what God says to them as they study the New Testament.

The Temptations of Jesus (Matt. 4:1-11)
Ask a member to volunteer to recall the basic events of the temptation account.

Ask, What do the terms *Satan* and *Devil* mean? (an opponent who is an accuser)

As you name the three temptations, instruct the group to recall Jesus' response and the issue at stake.
- First Temptation: Stones into bread. Jesus' response; It is better to obey God than to eat. The issue: obedience to God.
- Second Temptation: Put God's love to a test. Jesus' response: One does not have to test God to prove God's love. The issue: trusting God in spite of what others say.
- Third Temptation: Worship Satan to fulfill personal ambition. Jesus' response: God alone is worthy of worship. The issue: denial of personal ambition in favor of worshiping God alone.

---
[1] Henry T. Blackaby and Claude V. King, *Experiencing God: Knowing and Doing the Will of God* (Nashville: LifeWay Press, 1991) 111.

Ask the group the following questions related to the memorization of Scriptures:
- How do we know Jesus memorized the Scriptures?
- What did you notice about Jesus' response to Satan's use of the Scriptures? (Jesus quoted them back to him accurately).
- What Scriptures did Jesus memorize? (the Old Testament)

Have a member read Psalm 119:11, and ask, What does Jesus' memorization of the Scriptures say to us?

Ask the group the following question for thought: If we had only Scriptures we have committed to memory to teach, preach, and guide our church, how long could we function without repeating ourselves?

Principles of True Righteousness
Note that one of the themes in the Sermon on the Mount was Jesus' correcting the erroneous thinking of contemporary Judaism. Evidently they had taken the teachings of the Old Testament and interpreted them in such a way that their traditions which had evolved over centuries had become as important as God's Word. Ask the following questions:
- How do we know He was correcting the errors in their thinking and practice? (Jesus' use of the phrases "you have heard it said," or "it has been said," and "but I tell you")
- How do the Scriptures correct our thinking?

Principles of True Worship
Have the group scan the Scripture passage in Matthew 6:19-34. When they have finished, ask them:
- What things do you have in your home that are temporal (destined to perish)?
- What things do you have in your home that are eternal?
- What do you most often worry about—things that are temporal or things that are eternal?
- Which things do you most often pray about?

Principles of True Judgment
Have the person on your left state one of the principles of interpretation, for the Bible, then move to the next person on your left, and so on, until the five principles have been stated.

Read Matthew 7:1. Ask the group these questions:
- How can this verse, taken out of context, be misinterpreted? (It can be misinterpreted to mean the Christian has no right to engage in evaluating the truth of anything in any form.)
- What would be the result of such a belief in the day-to-day world? (moral and spiritual anarchy)
- What would be the result of such a belief in the churches? (toleration of false doctrine, evil, and an inability to confront sin when it arises in the church; churches would forget their commission to be positive agents of moral change in the world)

Instruct the group to apply the principles of "context" and "Scripture interprets Scripture" by comparing the following passages in their Bibles: Matthew 7:1-2; 1 Corinthians 5:12-13; Galatians 6:1-5.

Ask the group:
- How does looking at these illustrations help you understand judgment?
- What did Jesus mean in this passage? (James 4:12 states that God is the only Lawgiver and Judge. We should not judge in the sense of condemning people; however, we should evaluate all attitudes and activities of life by God's judgment—God's Word.)

Have the group turn in their member books to part 1 of "Responding To God's Word" on page 51. Discuss this activity using the following questions:
- What is the "rock" Jesus was speaking of in these verses? (obedience)
- How can we know we are obeying God's word?
- Why is an obedient lifestyle important to use when the "storms of life" come?
- What does Jesus' illustration about the builders say to us about the importance of our quiet time?

Peter's Confessions (Matt. 16:13-20)
Refer members to Matthew 16:13-20. Read the last paragraph on page 52 and the three interpretations from page 53 in the member's book appearing below.
1. Jesus referred to Himself as the rock.
2. Jesus referred to Simon's confession of faith as the rock.
3. Jesus referred to Simon Peter's leadership as the rock.

Ask, Why did the author lean toward the third interpretation? (answers given)
  a. It is the most natural.
  b. It suggests that Peter was the leader of the apostles and the early church.
  c. Paul used similar language to refer to Simon Peter and the other apostles.
  d. It is consistent with Peter's role in the early church.
  e. It is consistent with Peter's early ministry to Gentiles.

Ask the members what Jesus meant by "binding and loosing" in the context in which Jesus made the statement? (It had to do with our right to retain or forgive sins. Jesus was telling Peter that as he proclaimed the gospel of the kingdom, he could proclaim what had already been accomplished in heaven, and people would be loosed from their bondage to sin and unbelief.)

Read Matthew 16:24-26 to the group. Use the following questions to introduce the discussion on cross-bearing:
- What does it mean to deny self?
- What do people often mean when they speak of their cross?
- What is our cross? (cross spoke of death, thus death of our own wishes, desires, and so forth)

Reconciliation and Forgiveness (Matt. 18:15-35)
Have the group state the four steps to solving reconciliation problems. (See page 53 in member's book.)

Ask the group:
- Who is responsible for initiating reconciliation?
- Is it more difficult to initiate reconciliation when you have been offended or when you are the offender?
- What are some problems caused by not reconciling interpersonal problems with other people?
- What are some benefits of reconciliation?

Jesus' Teaching on Divorce (Matt. 19:1-12)
Ask the group to think for a few moments about the relationship between reconciliation and forgiveness and the problem of divorce. Ask, What impact would the following have on our marriages?
- living the principle of true righteousness from the Sermon on the Mount
- living in obedience to Christ as He reveals His will in His Word
- denial of oneself in favor of loving Christ and others
- exercising the principles of forgiveness and reconciliation in all our relationships

Have members refer to their Bible study worksheets. As time permits, lead the group to discuss the things God said to them during the week as they studied.

CONCLUSION—10 MINUTES

1. Preview next week's materials. Ask members to look at the unit overview appearing at the beginning of unit 4. Next week they will be studying the Gospel of Mark, with particular attention to Jesus' Early and Galilean ministry.

2. Again, remind members of the importance of doing the work. Encourage them to make time to daily work in their member book and to spend time with the Lord each day of the week.

AFTER THE SESSION

1. Carefully evaluate the effectiveness of the session. Use the questions that appear on page 11 in the course administrative plan to guide your evaluation.

2. Save materials you have developed for use in future groups of *Step by Step Through the New Testament*.

3. Immediately begin your preparations for next week's session.

4. Pray for the group. This week you will want to pray for their ability to hear God speak in the pages of the New Testament.

GROUP SESSION 4 — The Gospel of Mark

SESSION GOALS

 At the conclusion of this session members will:

1. Recall the significant facts about John Mark and his Gospel.

2. State lifestyle adjustments that may be required when a person follows Jesus.

3. Explain ways we can honor the Sabbath principle.

4. Express the root issue in the life of the Rich Young Man.

5. Define *greatness* using Jesus' definition.

Before the Session

❑ 1. Study carefully unit 4 and complete all learning activities. Review the group session goals above.

❑ 2. Pray for God's guidance as you prepare for this group session. Pray specifically for each member of your group.

❑ 3. Read through "During the Session." You may not have time in the session to cover all the questions in your Leader Guide. Ask God to guide you to the questions He wants discussed with the group. Decide on the amount of time to allow for each segment of the Bible study. Write in the margin of your Leader Guide the time you want each segment to begin.

❑ 4. Gather copies of the unit review quiz to pass out to group members.

❑ 5. Do the outside reading you feel necessary to acquaint yourself with unfamiliar subjects. You may want to do some extra reading on demonism and the blasphemy of the Holy Spirit.

❑ 6. Provide for refreshments if they are being served during the break.

During the Session

Part I
OPENING ACTIVITIES—20 MINUTES

1. Welcome members and begin with prayer. (5 min.)

2. Distribute and have members complete the unit review quiz. When they have finished, lead a discussion of their answers. (10 mins.) Quiz Answers: 1-D, 2-B, 3-A, 4-C.

Part II
BIBLE STUDY AND GROUP DISCUSSION—50 MINUTES

The Gospel of Mark
Instruct members to look at unit 4, page 59, before you begin the discussion. Have them recall the following information as you introduce the Book of Mark.

a. What are the distinct characteristics of Mark's Gospel? (You may refer to the introduction on page 59 for the answers.)

b. What are the commonly accepted evidences for John Mark's authorship of this book? (testimony of the early church and the early Christian leaders)

c. What significant facts did you learn about Mark's background? (grew up in an affluent Christian home, was a cousin to Barnabas)

d. What are the themes that are prominent in this book? (Importance of preaching and believing the gospel, presented Jesus as the Son of God, and emphasized Jesus' commitment to die for our redemption)

e. What is the correlation between Mark, Matthew, and Luke? (Mark was probably the first Gospel written, which means Matthew and Luke probably had it in hand when writing their accounts. Those two gospels quote many passages in Mark word for word).

f. Why do we think the Book of Mark may have been written for Roman readers? (Because he occasionally explained Greek expressions by their Latin equivalents, and he translated some Aramaic expressions to be sure Romans could understand them.)

Jesus' Early and Galilean Ministry
Ask the group to recall the beginning of Jesus' early and Galilean ministries (Mark 1:1-14, Early Ministry; Mark 2:1—9:50, Ministry in Galilee)

The Call of the First Disciples (Mark 1:16-20)
Have the members turn to day 3, page 64, in their books and Mark 1:16-20 in their Bibles, as they begin their discussion of the key passages. Use the following questions to discuss and apply the content of the study.
- What were the names of the first disciples who followed Jesus?
- What in the life of these men indicated their faith in Christ?

Read this quote from page 64 in the member's book: "When Jesus called them to be His disciples, they already were convinced that making disciples out of men was more important than looking for fish. Peter, Andrew, James, and John left their fishing business to follow Jesus."

Ask the group the following questions:
- What kind of adjustments did these men make to follow Jesus?
- What other biblical examples of people who followed Jesus can you recall?
- What do you think of when you consider "following Jesus?"
- Will Jesus ever ask you to make the same type adjustments these men made to follow Him?

The Healing of the Demoniac (Mark 1:21-28)
Have the group respond to the following questions related to this passage.
- What was the source of amazement to the people as they listened to Jesus teach? (His authority)
- How did Jesus deal with the person possessed of the demon? (spoke and cast it out)
- How do you think Jesus felt dealing with the evil He confronted? (He knew it existed, accepted the reality of it, and dealt with it decisively in God's power. He was not intimidated by the evil He encountered.)
- What does this say to us about facing evil in our community or nation?

Lord of the Sabbath (Mark 2:23—3:6)
Mention to the group that the Jewish Sabbath fell on what we now call Saturday. Ask the group:

What was the source of the Pharisees' complaint about Jesus' Sabbath conduct? (He violated their interpretation of how the Sabbath was to be observed.)

What was Jesus' response to their charge of unlawful actions? (Refer the group to Exodus 35:2: "For six days, work is to be done, but the seventh day shall be your holy day, a Sabbath of rest to the Lord. Whoever does any work on it must be put to death.")

Ask the group, What does that verse say to us? (Answers may vary, but the group should certainly agree the time we set aside for God should be a priority time for us).

Tell the group that even though we worship on Sunday, which is the first day of the week, we can still apply the "Sabbath principle" to our lives.

The Blasphemy of the Holy Spirit (Mark 3:20-30)
Ask the group, What was Jesus' response to the charge of casting out demons in the power of Satan? (It is illogical. Jesus is more powerful than Satan, and such accusation bordered on blasphemy of the Holy Spirit.)

Ask the group, If Jesus considered attributing the work of God to Satan as blasphemy, what do you think we can conclude about the blasphemy of the Holy Spirit?

The Feeding of the Five Thousand (Mark 6:30-44)
Ask, What significant fact did you learn about the feeding of the five thousand? (It is the only miracle recorded by all four gospel writers.)

Have a member recall the events of the feeding of the five thousand.
- How did the disciples feel to see the five thousand hungry? (see vv. 35-36)
- How did Jesus feel to see the five thousand hungry? (see vv. 34,37)

Cleanness and Corban (Mark 7:1-23)
Ask a member to explain what is known about the practice of "Corban."

Ask, How are we guilty of using religious practices as a veil for selfish indulgence?

Ask the group if they can think of contemporary religious traditions that violate God's law.

Refer the group to the activity based on Mark 7:14-23 (p. 68). Read and complete the statements making sure the members have the correct responses.

The Rich Young Man (Mark 10:17-22)
Refer the group to Mark 10:17-22, the account of the wealthy young man. Ask the group:
- What lessons did you draw from this passage?
- What was the "hardest issue" facing the young man? (surrender to Jesus' will)
- Is this the "hardest issue" facing us today?

The Desire for Greatness of James and John (Mark 10:35-45)
Have the group turn to page 70 in their books and ask,
- Was anything wrong with James' and John's request?
- Why did Jesus refuse to grant it?
- How did the other disciples respond?
- What one word could we say Jesus used to define greatness? (servanthood)
- How does this compare to the world's definition of greatness?

CONCLUSION—10 MINUTES

1. Preview next week's materials. Ask members to look at the unit overview appearing at the beginning of unit 5. Next week they will be studying the Gospel of Luke, with particular attention to Jesus' journey to Jerusalem.

2. Instruct members to pay particular attention to the travel itinerary as they complete the next unit. Much of the material Luke included in his account of the journey to Jerusalem does not appear in the the other gospels.

After the Session

1. Carefully evaluate the effectiveness of the session. Use the questions that appear on page 11 in the course administrative plan to guide your evaluation.

2. Save materials you have developed for use in future groups of *Step by Step Through the New Testament*.

3. Begin your preparations for next week's session.

4. Pray for the group. This week you will want to pray for them to be gripped by a vision of the dynamic change Jesus brings to the lives of those who follow Him.

GROUP SESSION 5 — The Gospel of Luke

SESSION GOALS

 At the conclusion of this session members will be able to:

1. Recall significant background material about the Gospel of Luke.

2. List facts about the birth of Jesus which only Luke records.

3. State the primary truth of select parables.

4. Outline the major events of the final weeks of Jesus' life.

5. State evidences for the resurrection of Jesus.

Before the Session

❑ 1. Study carefully unit 5 and complete all learning activities. Review the group session goals above.

❑ 2. Pray for God's guidance as you prepare for this group session. Pray specifically for each member of your group.

❑ 3. Read through "During the Session." You may not have time in the session to cover all the questions in your Leader Guide. Ask God to guide you to the questions He wants discussed with the group. Decide on the amount of time to allow for each segment of the Bible study. Write in the margin of your Leader Guide the time you want each segment to begin.

❑ 4. Gather copies of the unit review quiz to pass out to group members.

❑ 5. Provide for refreshments if they are being served during the break.

During the Session

Part I
OPENING ACTIVITIES—20 MINUTES

1. Welcome members and begin with prayer. (5 min.)

2. Distribute and have members complete the unit review quiz. When they have finished, lead a discussion of their answers. (10 mins.) Quiz Answers: 1-I, 2-G, 3-H, 4-C, 5-F, 6-D, 7-A, 8-B, 9-E, 10-J.

Part II
BIBLE STUDY AND GROUP DISCUSSION—50 MINUTES

The Background to Luke's Gospel
Use the following questions to begin your Bible study of the Gospel of Luke.

- What significant facts did you learn about the author's background? (the only Gentile writer in the NT, companion of the apostle Paul, a physician by training and vocation, also wrote the Book of Acts)

- What similarity do the opening verses in Luke share with Acts? (both writings have a dedication to Luke's friend, Theophilus, see Luke 1:3; Acts 1:1)

- What are the themes that are prominent in this book? (the Savior seeking the lost, strengthening the faith of the readers, reaching the outcasts and Gentiles)

- Why do we think the Book of Luke may have been written to strengthen Gentile Christians in their faith? (the salutation is to a Gentile. There is an emphasis on Jesus' ministry to Gentiles, women, and outcasts.)

Unique Facts About Jesus' Birth (Luke 1:5-25)
Have the group recall the unique facts of Jesus' birth as recorded by Luke. (near the time of John the Baptist's

birth, firmly linked to specific historical time frame, visit of the shepherds, visit to the temple when one week old)

Refer the group to Luke 1:5-25. Use the following questions to discuss the announcement of the birth of John the Baptist.
- What was the message to Zechariah and Elizabeth?
- How did Zechariah respond?
- What was the result of his doubt?
- What was the eventual outcome in their lives?
- In what ways can our disbelief affect our lives?
- When John was born, what happened in their lives?

Jesus' Baptism (3:21-22)
1. Have the group recall what they learned about John the Baptist.
2. Ask, Why did Jesus insist on being baptized? (as a means of identifying with sinful human beings and as a pledge of His commitment to do God's will)
3. Why are we baptized? (to identify with Christ and indicate our surrender to God's will)

Jesus at Simon's Home (7:36-50)
Have a member relate the events of Luke 7:40-50.

Ask the following questions:
- Why do you think Simon invited Jesus to his home?
- How do you feel about Simon's judgment of Jesus? (his condemnation for allowing the woman to touch His feet)
- Are we ever guilty of mistakes in our relationships with others? (by judging them on the basis of appearances only)
- What is the main point of the parable? (Jesus told a parable of God's forgiveness.)

The Good Samaritan (10:25-37)
Have the group open their Bibles to Luke 10:25-37. Have a member tell the basic story of the parable of The Good Samaritan. Mention to the group that most parables have one main point or principle as the central message Jesus wanted to get across to His listeners. Then, ask the following questions as you discuss this parable.
- Why did Jesus answer the scribe's question with a question? (Jesus' questions usually were designed to probe and help that person think.)
- How did Jesus' parable challenge the stereotypes in the minds of the audience?
- What is the point of the parable? (Our neighbor is any person we see in need.)
- Ask the group what Christian ministries they know of that minister to persons such as the man on the road.

The Rich Fool (12:13-21)
As you begin, have the group turn to page 83 in their books to discuss the parable of the rich fool. Read Dr. Lea's statements appearing on page 83; "God could call the man 'Fool' because the man assumed that he controlled the future. He did not consider that all that was important to him could vanish in a moment."

Ask the group the following questions:
1. What do you value most in life?
2. Do your values reflect God's wisdom or the Rich Fool's shortsightedness?
3. If you were fleeing an approaching storm and knew that God would grant you one thing, what would you choose?

Encourage them to look over these values once more in their next personal quiet time with the Lord.

The Parable of the Lost (Prodigal) Son (15:11-24)
Have a member tell the story of the prodigal son. Then ask the following questions:
- What had to happen before the son could be restored to his father?
- What was the problem faced by the older son?
- What two primary truths did you learn in this parable? (The love of the Father for us even when we sin overwhelms and encourages us. And, we find true fulfillment only by living daily in the will of the Father.)

Ask the group, Can you think of someone whose rebellion against God has cost him/her dearly? (It is not necessary to share these names.) Does the prodigal son/daughter you have thought of have any hope for turning life around?

The Rich Man and Lazarus (16:19-31)
Have a member tell the basic story of this parable. Then ask the following questions:

- What was the meaning of Lazarus' name? (God is his help.)
- What does this parable say to us about the importance of following and serving Christ now? (After death will be too late to make such a choice.)
- What did you see that indicated that even in hell the rich man failed to see the essential difference between himself and Lazarus? (He wanted Lazarus to wait on him by cooling his torment with a drink of water.)
- What was the primary message of this parable?

Jesus' Final Week

Beginning with Palm Sunday, have members recall the events that occurred during the week. As you state the day, they should recall the events. (If they have trouble outlining Jesus' final week, instruct them to turn back to unit 2, pp. 37-41, for help.)

Gethsemane (Luke 22:41-44)

Refer the group to Luke 22:41-44 in their Bibles. Briefly recount the events for the group. Read the author's statement on page 87: "Jesus wanted to do God's will more than He wanted to escape death." Ask the group the following questions:
- Would Jesus ever ask us to do anything He had not done?
- Would Jesus ever ask us to die for Him?
- Where do we expend most of our time, effort, and anxiety?
- Allow the members to surface other insights they have gained from the accounts of Jesus' final days.

The Trial and Crucifixion of Jesus (22:54—23:49)

Have a member offer a summary of Jesus' trial. Be sure the principle characters are included. Note that the members will spend some time studying the reinstatement of Peter in the next unit. Ask the following:
- What was wrong with Jesus' trial? (He was accused by false witnesses. In violation of Jewish law, the trial was held at night, and Jesus was convicted by His own testimony. He was brutalized by the authorities and handed over by the Roman governor as the result of coercion by a mob.)
- Which disciple did not desert Jesus? (John)
- Thinking about Pilate, how do people still sell their integrity to gain favor of people?
- What can we conclude from the attitudes of the two thieves on the cross?
- What can we conclude from the response of Jesus to the repentant thief?

The Burial, Resurrection, and Ascension of Jesus (24:1-53)

Have a member recall the account of the resurrection. Ask them the following questions:
- How long did Jesus remain in the tomb? (Friday to Sunday—He arose on the third day.)
- Where was Jesus buried? (in the borrowed tomb of Joseph of Arimathea)
- What safeguards were taken to insure His body did not disappear?
- Who discovered His body was gone?
- What can we consider as evidences of the resurrection? (the empty tomb, the testimony of the apostles and the early church, the very existence of the early church, the witness of the Holy Spirit and the written word of God)
- Which post-resurrection appearances do you recall?

CONCLUSION—10 MINUTES

Preview next week's materials. Instruct members to look at the unit overview appearing at the beginning of unit 6 on page 90. Next week they will be studying the Gospel of John.

After the Session

1. Carefully evaluate the effectiveness of the session. Use the questions that appear on page 11 in the course administrative plan to guide your evaluation.
2. Save any materials you have developed for use in future groups of *Step by Step Through the New Testament*.
3. Immediately begin your preparations for next week's session.
4. Pray for the group. This week you will want to pray for their willingness to choose those priorities for their lives that honor God.

GROUP SESSION 6 — The Gospel of John

SESSION GOALS

 At the conclusion of this session members will be able to:

1. State the purpose of John's Gospel.

2. List at least four of Jesus' "I am" statements.

3. Mention the special characteristics of John's Gospel.

4. Define what it means to be "born again."

5. List three truths based on John 13:34-35.

6. Explain the relationship between abiding in Christ and obeying Christ.

Before the Session

❑ 1. Study carefully unit 6 and complete all learning activities. Review the group session goals above.

❑ 2. Pray for God's guidance as you prepare for this group session and for each group member.

❑ 3. Read through "During the Session." You may not have time to cover all the questions in your Leader Guide. Ask God to guide you to the questions He wants discussed with the group. Decide on how much time to allow for each segment of Bible study. and write in your Leader Guide the time you want each segment to begin.

❑ 4. Photocopy the unit review quiz for each member.

During the Session

Part I
OPENING ACTIVITIES —20 MINUTES

1. Welcome members and begin with prayer. (5 min.)

2. Distribute and have members complete the unit review quiz. When they have finished, lead a discussion of their answers. (10 mins.) Quiz Answers: 1-E, 2-C, 3-A, 4-H, 5-J, 6-F, 7-D, 8-B, 9-I, 10-G.

Part II
BIBLE STUDY AND GROUP DISCUSSION— 40 MINUTES

John's Gospel
Have the group recall the following information as you begin the Bible study.

1. What is unique about John's gospel? (See p. 91 in the member's book. He emphasizes the person and deity of Christ, wrote with a deep awareness of theology, and elaborated on the importance of Jesus' incarnation. John made clear that Jesus' public ministry lasted longer than a single year, and he also preserved many of Jesus' significant speeches.)

2. What significant facts did you learn about John's background? (He was a Jew who wrote in a Jewish style. He is referred to in the Gospel as "the disciple whom Jesus loved.")

3. Why does this Gospel stand apart from the other three Synoptic Gospels? (It includes material the Synoptic Gospels did not include. It shows that Jesus' public ministry lasted over two years, and probably more than three. It is not as concerned with a chronology of Jesus' life as with emphasizing aspects of his ministry; see member's book, p. 90.)

4. What are the themes that are prominent in this book? (light and darkness, faith and belief, love, Jesus' deity and miracles)

5. Why do we think the Book of John may have been written for young Christians and those curious about Christianity? (His stated purpose in John 20:31 was to help people know about Jesus and believe in Him.)

Beholding Jesus' Glory: The Eternal Word Incarnate (1:1-18)
Begin with the person to your left and have the group name the seven signs in John's Gospel. If they cannot recall, refer them to the member's book, (p. 94.)

Read John 1:1 and John 1:14 to the group. Then ask, What is the uniqueness of John's claim in these two verses? (the Word existed before time, was distinct from God the Father, and Jesus was the living Word, p. 95).

Ask the group to recall the meaning of grace and truth. (Grace referred to God's steadfast love. Truth referred to God's complete reliability.)

Begin with the person to your right and have the group recall the seven "I AM" sayings in John's Gospel. Refer the group to page 94 if they need help. Ask members to state one truth they gained from looking at the "I AM" statements.

Nicodemus' Conversion (3:1-15)
Ask a member to share the essential facts related to Jesus' encounter with Nicodemus. Then, ask the following:
- What is the correct understanding of "born again?" (to be born from above, or to be born of the Spirit)
- Why do we believe Nicodemus became a follower of Jesus? (He spoke in a subtle defense of Jesus, John 7:50-52. He later helped Joseph of Arimathea in the burial of Jesus' body, John 19:39.)
- What can the manner in which Jesus responded to Nicodemus say to us in our witness to the inquiring?

Questions About Manuscripts: the Account of the Woman Caught in Adultery
Ask, What have been your thoughts as you considered the variations in the accounts of Jesus' life in the Gospels? (By now the group members will have picked up on the occasional differences in the Synoptic Gospels and the noticeable differences between those and John's Gospel).

Allow time for members to surface questions related to this subject. Mention to them *The Doctrine of the Bible* by David S. Dockery. This work addresses in general terms questions about the authenticity and reliability of the Scriptures.

In your brief explanation at this point, you may choose to include in this segment of the discussion of the following statements from *The Doctrine of the Bible*. (The leader's guide material in this section is based on statements in *The Doctrine of the Bible* by David S. Dockery. Since the focus of the group session is to examine the Gospel of John, as opposed to the doctrine of the Bible, defer lengthy discussions to a more convenient time).

a. "There are more than five thousand manuscripts of the New Testament, making the New Testament the best-attested document among all ancient writings."[1]

b. Dockery quotes F. F. Bruce: "Perhaps we can appreciate how wealthy the New Testament is in manuscript attestation if we compare the textual material for other ancient historical works. For Caesar's Gallic War (composed between 58 and 50 BC) there are several extant MSS (manuscripts), but only nine or ten are good, and the oldest is some 900 years later than Caesar's day."[2]

c. In concluding, mention to the members that while we do not possess (to our knowledge) the original copies of the Scriptures, "When we read our present translations, we can read with the assurance that they faithfully represent the original sources. Also, we believe that they include not more or less than the writings God purposed to include in the canonical Scriptures."[3]

---
[1] David S. Dockery, *The Doctrine of the Bible* (Nashville: Convention Press, 1991), 99.
[2] F.F. Bruce, *The New Testament Documents: Are They Reliable?* (London: The InterVarsity Fellowship, 1961), 16.
[3] Dockery, *The Doctrine of the Bible,* 107.

The Doctrine of the Bible contains extensive endnotes and a bibliography. You may suggest Dockery's work to those who want to follow up on the subject.

Jesus' View Toward Sin (7:53—8:11)

Have a member tell the basic story of the woman caught in adultery. Then ask the following questions as you discuss this passage:
- Why did the Pharisees bring her forward? (to try and trap Jesus and discredit Him with the people)
- What was the hypocrisy of the accusers? (The law, Deut 22:22-24, required that both the man and woman be stoned—they only brought the woman.)
- Why did Jesus' answer confound them? (We do not know what He wrote in the sand, but whatever it was, it exposed their hypocrisy.)
- What was Jesus' charge to the woman? (to leave in peace and give up her sinful lifestyle)

The Eternity of Jesus (John 8:51-58)

Have the group scan John 8:51-58. Ask a member to share about Jesus' encounter with the Jews. Ask the following questions as you discuss this passage:
- Why was Jesus accused of being demon-possessed? (because He said that those who kept His word would never see death)
- What was the significance of Jesus' use of "I AM" in verse 58? (It was a clear claim to deity and thus to superiority over Abraham.)
- What is the relationship of this passage to the prologue (1:1-18) of this Gospel?
- What is the relationship of verse 58 to the seven "I AM" statements?

Does Sin Cause Suffering? (John 9:1-12)

Have a member briefly tell the story of the man born blind. Use the following questions to discuss the passage.
- Why is this such a crucial Scripture passage? (It talks about a possible relation between sin and suffering.)
- What did it say about the relationship between sin and the man's blindness? (Jesus first stated that the blindness was not due to sin, then added that the purpose was that a divine work might take place in him and reveal the glory of God.)
- Optional: What principle of interpretation applies in this instance? (Interpret difficult texts with help from clearer texts.)

Our Eternal Security (John 10:27-30)

Have the group turn in their Bible to John 10:27-30. After they look over the passage, ask the following questions:
- What is the passage's emphasis? (Eternal life is a gift we keep because Jesus holds us firmly in His grip.)
- What characteristics should begin to show in the life of a believer?

Love is Evidence of our Christian Faith (John 13:34-35)

Instruct the group to turn in their Bibles to John 13:34-35 and to page 101 in their books. As you begin the discussion, read John 13:34-35 to the group. Ask the following questions as you discuss the passage.
- In part "A" of the activity, what type spirit would those statements reveal in a person making them? (a cold, unloving spirit)
- In part "B" why is "loving one another as Christ loved" the only action that qualifies as correct?

Read the author's statement (p. 101), "Jesus' words here contain a command, a pattern, and a result." Ask,
- What is the command? (love one another)
- What is the pattern? (as Jesus loved the disciples)
- What is the result? (Onlookers will know the professed faith one has in Christ is real.)

Our Source of Spiritual Strength (15:1-10)

Have the group open their Bibles to John 15 as you begin the discussion. Ask the following questions as you discuss this passage:
- What words can you recall that would characterize what Jesus said in this passage?
- Why is "relationship" a key word that comes out of this passage? (A vital relationship with Christ is clearly spoken of as our source of spiritual strength.)
- What two words did Jesus use to show how we remain in relationship with Him? (abide and obey)
- What is the relationship between abiding in Christ and obeying Christ (15:10)? (We abide in proper relationship with Him through our obedience.)

The Holy Spirit and the World (16:5-11)

Have the group open their Bibles to John 16:5-11 and to pages 102-3 in their member books. As you begin the discussion, instruct them to look over the matching activity at the top of page 103. Ask the following:

- What is stated as actions the Holy Spirit will do? (He exposes sin, v. 9; He convicts the world of Christ's righteousness, v. 10; He shows that Satan has been judged and defeated v. 11.)
- How can this passage encourage us in witnessing?

Read John 16:13-14. Ask, How does this help us understand the Holy Spirit's role in our lives? (He will guide us as we understand and share the truth.)

Jesus' Words on the Cross: "It is Finished" (19:28-30)

Refer the group to John 19:28-30. Ask the following questions as you discuss this passage:
- How would you characterize the words "It is finished" in normal, everyday conversation?
- In what sense do you think Jesus used the phrase "It is finished"?
- What do Jesus' words "It is finished" say to us?

Thomas: A Pilgrimage of Faith (John 20:24-29)

Have a member briefly share with the group what he knows about the disciple named Thomas. Then ask the following questions as you discuss this segment:
- How are we like Thomas?
- Can you think of an Old Testament character who paralleled Thomas' pilgrimage in seeking visible proof of God's work? (Gideon, Judg. 6:17-22,36-40)
- Would you rather wrestle with doubting like Thomas or with failure like Peter?

Simon Peter: Restoring a Fallen Leader (21:15-19)

Ask the group to open their Bibles to John 21 as you begin the discussion. Briefly tell the facts in chapter 21. Ask, What previous events in Simon's life parallel the events of this passage?

1. Another miraculous catch of fish recorded at the time of Peter's call (Luke 5:4-11) parallels the catch in this passage (vv. 6-7).

2. Peter's three denials (Matt. 26:69-75; Mark 14:66-72; Luke 22:54-62; John 18:16-18, 25-27) of a relationship with Jesus are paralleled by the three questions Jesus asked Peter. The questions specifically addressed the nature of their relationship.

Note for the group that only John records this encounter in which Jesus reinstates Peter. Continue the discussion with the following questions:
  a. What is the meaning of the Greek word *agapao?* (a deep, unselfish love)
  b. What is the meaning of the Greek word *phileo?* (a friendship type love)
  c. Note for the group that the first two times Jesus questioned Simon he used the word *agapao*. The third time Jesus asked Simon if he loved Him He used *phileo*.
  d. Ask, What is the significance of Jesus' switching to Peter's word in the third question? (Simon, even if you only love me this much, feed my sheep.)
  e. What were the two commands Jesus gave to Simon? (feed My sheep and follow Me)
  f. Ask the members, What lessons in this passage can give us encouragement?

As time permits, lead the group to discuss the things God said to them during the week as they studied.

CONCLUSION—10 MINUTES

Preview next week's materials. Ask members to look at the unit overview appearing at the beginning of unit 7. Next week they will begin their study of the early church in the Book of Acts.

After the Session

1. Carefully evaluate the effectiveness of the session. Use the questions that appear on page 11 in the course administrative plan to guide your evaluation.

2. Save any materials you have developed for use in future groups of *Step by Step Through the New Testament*.

3. Immediately begin your preparations for next week's session.

4. Pray for the group. This week you will want to pray for their vision of how their church can become a platform for reaching out in world missions.

GROUP SESSION 7

The Book of Acts Part 1 (1-12)

SESSION GOALS

At the conclusion of this session members will be able to:

1. Explain why Luke is accepted as the author of Acts.

2. State one reason why Christians should respond thoughtfully to events happening around them.

3. List three characteristics of a spiritual church.

4. Define the pattern God used to lead the church in Jerusalem.

5. Express how new member training can help new converts in their church.

Before the Session

❏ 1. Study carefully unit 7 and complete all learning activities. Review the group session goals above.
❏ 2. Pray for God's guidance as you prepare for this group session. Pray specifically for each member.
❏ 3. Read "During the Session." You may not have time in the session to cover all the questions in your Leader Guide. Ask God to guide you to the ones He wants discussed with the group. Decide on the amount of time to allow for each segment of the Bible study. Write in the margin of your Leader Guide when to begin each segment.
❏ 4. Gather copies of the unit review quiz for each member.
❏ 5. Optional: Choose four key statements or truths from the Scripture passages or from the member book to be discussed by the group during the session. Write them on a large piece of paper or poster board and hang them on the wall or hand them out at an appropriate time for the members to discuss. (You will need to decide where to include this activity in the session.)
❏ 6. Provide for refreshments if they are being served during the break.

During the Session

Part I
OPENING ACTIVITIES—20 MINUTES

1. Welcome members and begin with prayer. (5 mins.)

2. Distribute and have members complete the unit review quiz. When they have finished, lead a discussion of their answers. (10 mins.) Quiz Answers: 1-F, 2-E, 3-G, 4-D, 5-H, 6-C, 7-I, 8-B, 9-J, 10-A.

Part II
BIBLE STUDY AND GROUP DISCUSSION—50 MINUTES

Introduction to Acts

The group has just completed a study of the Gospels. Ask a member to recount for the group what they learned about the connection between the Gospel of Luke and the Book of Acts. (Both were authored by the same person.)

The group may wonder why Luke and Acts do not appear together as a unit in the Scriptures. Remind them that as the canon developed, the accounts of Jesus' life were deemed most important, and thus were placed first in order of appearance.

Have the group recall the following information as you begin the Bible study.
  a. What are the distinct characteristics of Acts? (You may refer to the introduction on p. 107 for the answers.)

b. Ask a member to recall the two-fold division of Acts. (1. Progress of the Gospel Among Jews 1:1—12:25; 2. Progress of the Gospel Among Gentiles, 13:1—28:31)
c. Ask a member to tell the suggested alternative title for the Book of Acts. (The Acts of the Holy Spirit) Ask why this was suggested. (Acts traces the movement of the Holy Spirit into and through the lives of the church.)

Discuss Luke the physician being author of both the Gospel of Luke and the Book of Acts. You may want to use the following questions:
a. Why do we believe the same person authored both books? (Both are addressed to one certain Theophilus. They are similar in style and vocabulary.)
b. What are the commonly accepted evidences for Luke's authorship of this book? (Leaders in the early church agreed that Luke was the author of Acts. The author of Acts and the Third Gospel appear to be the same person. Both Luke and Acts are written in a similar style with the use of a cultured type of Greek. Both books have a similar interest in Gentiles and the work of the Holy Spirit. The author of Acts was a companion of Paul but was not a prominent New Testament character.)
c. What are some of the emphases seen in Acts? (the gospel began in the cradle of Judaism and moved steadfastly to the dominant city of the Roman Empire; the heroic achievements of the apostle Paul; the innocence of early Christians as they faced various false accusations)

The Trustworthiness of Acts
Note for the group that Luke is the only Gospel writer to present chronological information that allows us to date the period of the ministry of John the Baptist and also of Jesus (Luke 3:1-2). Ask the group why this is important.

Read Luke 1:1-4 to the group. Note for the group that Luke's own testimony is one of making careful inquiry to report the truth about Jesus. Read the author's statement appearing on page 110, "Luke always had his facts straight." Ask, What does Luke's example say to us as Christians living in a modern society? (We are to be well-informed, thoughtful Christian citizens.)

Optional Discussion Activity: The goal of this activity is to create in the group members a desire to act as responsible Christian citizens. Divide the group into two subgroups for the discussion segment.

The Situation: A phony petition is being circulated among churches in your area. The content of that (bogus) petition alleges that an unbeliever has petitioned the government to restrict, or if possible, ban any broadcasting of religious programming in your country. The petition instructs each concerned person to call or write a government agency and lodge a protest against this alleged plan.

Instructions:
1. Group A will discuss and report on the question, What would be an inappropriate response?
2. Group B will discuss and report on the question, What would be an appropriate Christian response? (Allow the groups five minutes to formulate a response.)
3. Call for reports. Allow each group two minutes to tell how they would respond. Allow five minutes for further discussion.
4. Conclude the activity with the following questions:
   - What could be the possible result of each type response?
   - How does an inappropriate response to problems in the church or in our community damage the church? (destroy credibility)
   - Why does a thoughtful, accurate response build credibility and offer a good witness for the church? (Remind the group that a foolish response can be as damaging to the credibility of the church as no response at all.)
5. If the following suggestions are not named as positive responses, mention them to the group.
   a. Concerned Christians can check with their local denominational executives to verify the authenticity of such rumors.
   b. Read the denominational newspaper. Such newspapers normally try to keep their readers informed about factual matters in the government and social agencies. Editors will also try to inform readers of such items of interest.
   c. Investigate to see if responsible plans of action are being conducted by local or national denominational groups before formulating our own response.

It may then be possible to add one's effort to such action.

6. Ask the group, What teaching of Jesus comes to mind as you have thought through this situation? (If no one recalls the verse, conclude this segment by reading from Matthew 10:16, "I am sending you out like sheep among wolves. Therefore be as shrewd as snakes and as innocent as doves.")

Select Passages From Acts 1—12

The Departure of Jesus and the Arrival of the Holy Spirit (1:9—2:41)
Ask these questions as you discuss the ascension of Jesus and the coming of the Holy Spirit at Pentecost:
- What happened in the account of Jesus' ascension?
- What were the two promises given by the angels at the ascension? (Jesus would now reside in heaven, and would return in a manner similar to the way they had seen Him depart.)

Have a member tell what happened at Pentecost. Then ask the following questions:
- What did the fire symbolize to the Jews? (Fire as a symbol of the divine presence was common among the Jews.)
- What did you learn about the speaking in tongues? (The words spoken in "tongues" were recognized by the listeners in their own languages. Have a member turn to Acts 2:8 and count the number of languages or dialects. Depending on the translation they are using they should find reference to 15 or 16 known languages or dialects.)
- How did the crowd respond to the events as Peter preached? (Some believed and some were skeptical.)
- What were the four elements of Peter's sermon? (1) He responded with a rebuttal to the charge of drunkenness among the disciples, 2:14-15. (2) He explained what the noise, sight, and speaking in tongues indicated, 2:16-21. (3) He presented Jesus' life, death, and resurrection as the apex of divine action for our salvation, 2:22-36. (4) He concluded with an appeal to the people to surrender their lives to Christ, 2:37-39.

Characteristics of a Spiritual Church (2:42-47)
Ask the group to name characteristics of a spiritual church. As they name them, write them on a board or large piece of paper. Instruct the members to turn to page 116 in their member books, and look at the characteristics in activity B. Ask, What three characteristics in this list are most important to you?

Ask the group to think a moment about the Gospels. Have them recall Scripture passages from Jesus' life that illustrate the characteristics of a spiritual church.

Ask, If a first-time visitor were to be interviewed after visiting your congregation, what words would he use to describe the church?

Ask, What actions can we take to strengthen the spiritual life of our church?

The Church Praying and Facing Adversity (4:23-31)
Have a member share with the group what happened in this passage of Scripture. Ask the following questions as you discuss this passage:
- Have any of you ever been ostracized or threatened because you are a Christian?
- How did the church in Acts respond? (prayer and praise)
- Which did their prayer major on, praise or petition? (praise)
- What does this imply for our prayer life?
- What did you learn about Satan's approach to attack the church? (Satan often attacks the church using a dual approach, persecution from without, and deception and division from within.)

Refer the group to Acts 5:1-11. Have a member tell about Ananias and Sapphira. Use the following questions as you discuss this passage:
- What was their sin?
- Why did God deal with it so severely?
- What relationship can you see between their sin and blasphemy of the Holy Spirit. (labeling the lies and corruption of their own hearts as the will of God)

Have a member tell about the problem that developed in the ministry to the widows (Acts 6:1-7). Use the following questions as you discuss this passage:
- What were the two types of widows in the church? (Hebrew and Grecian)

- What was the problem that developed? (Grecian widows were being overlooked)

Ask the group to outline the procedure by which the problem was resolved in the Jerusalem church. As they need help you may share the following outline.
1. The leadership became aware of the need.
2. The leadership called the church together to inform them and seek God's will.
3. The Holy Spirit led the church to respond.
4. The church experienced God's power and was strengthened as it followed God's leadership.

Ask the group the following questions related to this passage:[1]
a. How does your church body discern the will of God?
b. How does your church body address problems?
c. What does this passage say to how any church should deal with issues that arise?

Simon the Sorcerer (8:5-24)

Instruct the group to open their Bibles to Acts 8:5-24. As you begin the discussion, have a member share with the group about the conversion of Simon the Sorcerer. Use the following questions to discuss the passage:
1. First, assume Simon was not really saved. What needed to happen in his life? (conversion)
2. Next, assume Simon was genuinely converted:
   a. What evidences are there in the passage that Simon was truly converted?
   b. What type of adjustments in his relationship to those around him was he experiencing?
   c. What was the chief temptation Simon was dealing with? (to exercise power)
   d. Why do you think Simon tried to "purchase" the ability of the apostles to bestow the Holy Spirit on other believers? (Answers may vary, but acting in the strength of known resources was the only way he knew to do things.)

Remind the group that experiencing conversion does not mean one automatically knows how to live as a Christian. Ask the group:
- Can you think of the names of churches in the New Testament Scriptures that gave evidence of spiritual immaturity? (nearly all of them)
- What should reasonably be expected of new believers?
- How should the church respond when new believers exhibit unchristian behaviors?
- What can the local church do to assist new members in learning to effectively live the Christian life?

CONCLUSION—10 MINUTES

1. Preview next week's materials. Ask members to look at the unit overview appearing at the beginning of unit 8. Next week they will complete their study of the Book of Acts.

2. Optional: Assign the following topics, one per member, to be reported on in the next session.
   - Paul's early life and background
   - Paul's conversion
   - The conversion of Cornelius
   - Paul's missionary journeys
   - The Jerusalem Council
   - Paul's voyage to Rome

If they will be comfortable with the assignment, select members who have not previously been called on for this type activity. Reports must be limited to a two-minute summary.

After the Session

1. Carefully evaluate the effectiveness of the session. Use the questions that appear on page 11 in the course administrative plan to guide your evaluation.

2. Save any materials you have developed for use in future groups of *Step by Step Through the New Testament*.

3. Immediately begin your preparations for next week's session.

4. Pray for the group. This week you will want to pray for the members to realize how God uses ordinary life to prepare them for extraordinary service.

---

[1]This series of questions was adapted from content in the course *Experiencing God: Knowing and Doing the Will of God*, by Henry T. Blackaby and Claude V. King. (Nashville: LifeWay Press, 1990), 168.

GROUP SESSION 8

The Book of Acts Part 2 (13-28)

SESSION GOALS

At the conclusion of this session members will be able to:

1. Discuss knowledgeably the life and ministry of the apostle Paul.

2. State principles for solving problems from the Jerusalem Council.

3. Express one reason the gospel causes conflict with the ungodly.

4. Sense the need to share the gospel with the lost.

Before the Session

❑ 1. Study carefully unit 8 and complete all learning activities. Review the group session goals above.

❑ 2. Pray for God's guidance as you prepare for this group session. Pray specifically for each member of your group.

❑ 3. Read through "During the Session." You may not have time in the session to cover all the questions in your Leader Guide. Ask God to guide you to the questions He wants discussed with the group. Decide on the amount of time to allow for each segment of the Bible study. Write in the margin of your Leader Guide the time you want each segment to begin.

❑ 4. Make each member a copy of the unit review quiz.

❑ 5. Optional: Choose four key statements or truths from the Scripture passages or from the member book to be discussed by the group during the session. Write them on a large piece of paper or poster board and hang them on the wall or hand them out at an appropriate time for the members to discuss. (You will need to decide where to include this activity in the session.)

❑ 6. Provide for refreshments if they are being served during the break.

During the Session

Part I
OPENING ACTIVITIES—20 MINUTES

1. Welcome members and begin with prayer. (5 mins.)

2. Distribute and have members complete the unit review quiz. When they have finished, lead a discussion of their answers. (10 mins.) Quiz Answers: 1-E, 2-I, 3-F, 4-B, 5-C, 6-G, 7-I, 8-A, 9-D, 10-H.

Part II
BIBLE STUDY AND GROUP DISCUSSION—40 MINUTES

As you begin, read John 17:17, "Sanctify them by the truth; your word is truth." Tell the group that Jesus was praying for the disciples, and as He prayed He mentioned the truthfulness of the Word of God.

Casually hold out your Bible and ask, Do you believe this—all of it—is the Word of God? After the group responds, make this statement: Say, Acts 1:8 is part of God's Word. Are we accountable to obey it?

Read or quote Acts 1:8 to the group. Then have a member point out on the map how the progress of the spread of the gospel is outlined in that verse.

Saul the Pharisee—Paul the Apostle

Mention to the group that after Acts 13:9 the name Saul was dropped and the apostle was always referred to as Paul. For the sake of simplicity we will use Paul.

Instruct the group to open their Bibles to Acts 9 as you begin the discussion. Tell the group the ministry of Paul dominates the majority of the book of Acts. At this time call for reports on Paul.
 a. Have the assigned members share about Paul's background.
 b. Ask the second person to give the report on Paul's conversion.

Have the group think for a moment about Ananias. Then ask the following questions.
- Why was Ananias afraid to go to Paul?
- How did God reassure him?
- How did Ananias then respond?
- What was the result of his ministry to Paul?
- What do you admire most about Ananias?

Note for the group that even though Ananias had reservations, he nonetheless trusted and immediately obeyed God. Ask the group to discuss this statement: Delayed obedience is disobedience.
 a. Why is this true or not true?
 b. Can you think of other characters in the Bible who faced intimidating assignments?
 c. Were they immediately obedient or did they stall at God's command?
 d. If they stalled, how did their hesitation limit or hinder them later?

(If the group cannot think of anyone right away, refer them to Moses, Exodus 3 and 4. Apply the questions to his story.)

Conclude this discussion by reminding the group that it is better to hesitate and later obey than it is to promise obedience and never obey. Jesus spoke to this in the Parable of the Two Sons: Matthew 21:28-32.

Shaped for God's Service

Read the author's statement appearing on page 124 "Just as God used Paul's background to prepare him for ministry, God will use our backgrounds in preparing us to carry out unique tasks for His glory."

Ask the group to recall examples in the Scriptures of how God used things that happened in other persons' lives to prepare them for His service. (Some possibilities are Joseph's being sold by his brothers, Moses, Gideon, David, Jonah, Nehemiah.)

Ask, Can any of you share how God has used things that have happened in your life to minister to others? (Allow time for members to respond as they feel comfortable.)

The First Gentile Convert: Cornelius (Acts 10)

Have the group open their Bibles to Acts 10. As you begin the discussion, have the member assigned give the summary of Cornelius' and his family being converted. You can be sure the following information is mentioned by asking the questions as necessary:
- Why was the story of Cornelius unique? (It is the first record of a Gentile convert.)
- What was Cornelius's occupation?
- What was he recognized for by the community?

Have the group look at the activity appearing on page 125. Ask question B, "If you knew a person like Cornelius today, what would you assume about that person?" After the group responds, ask these questions from page 125:
 a. Question C: "Had Cornelius died the day before he had a vision, what would have been his eternal destiny?" (He would have gone to hell.)
 b. Question D: "Why did the angel tell Cornelius to send for Peter rather than directly telling him how to be saved?" (God uses human instruments.)

Say, We have agreed that the Bible is the Word of God, and we know God's Word is true. So then, what should Cornelius' story say to us about our evangelism?

Say, If we say we believe the gospel and do not share the gospel, do we really believe the gospel?

Discuss Simon Peter's Role in Cornelius' Conversion

Briefly review for the group the account of Simon's vision on the rooftop. Ask the following questions as you discuss that event:
- Why was Peter reluctant to accept the vision God gave him?
- How did the Lord respond to Peter's reluctance?

- Has God ever called you to do something you did not want to do?
- What happened after you obeyed?

Paul's First Missionary Journey (13—14)
Note the path of the first missionary journey on the map. Then read Acts 13:1-5 to the group.

As you introduce the missionary journeys, ask the group to discuss the following statement: Everyone who is saved also is called to serve. The following questions may help generate the discussion.
- If you agree, why? On what Scripture can you base your answer?
- If you disagree, why? On what Scripture can you base your answer?

Tell the group the statement is true. At the point of conversion every believer receives a call to service.

Ask the group the following questions:
- Who accompanied Paul on the first missionary journey? (Barnabas, Acts 13:2)
- Where did Paul usually proclaim Christ first in the cities he visited?
- How were Paul and Barnabas received by those who heard the gospel? (Some believed, others did not. The unbelieving Jews were consistently filled with jealousy and persecuted them.)
- Were the unbelieving Jews more concerned with lives being changed by an encounter with God or with retaining their positions and power?
- How does the encounter between Paul and the Jews challenge us as we experience growth in our local congregations?

The Jerusalem Council (15:1-29)
Call on the assigned member to briefly summarize the events of the Jerusalem Council.

Ask the group to recall the three results of the Council of Jerusalem. (Circumcision and obeying the Mosaic law were not necessary for salvation. Gentile Christians were to abstain from certain practices for the sake of Jewish-Gentile relationships within the church. The church maintained a unity which gave credibility to its witness of the gospel.)

Ask, What principles can we draw from this to guide us in our churches? If the group has difficulty with this, some suggested responses are:
a. Hear differing viewpoints calmly.
b. Look for what God is doing.
c. Adjust our attitudes, opinions, and lives to be in alignment with the Scriptures.
d. Recognize that God can bring the church to a harmonious resolution of crisis without division in the body of Christ.

Paul's Second Missionary Journey (15:36—18:22)
Call attention to the map. Note the path of Paul's second missionary journey. Refer the group to Acts 15:36-41 and read the passage. Ask the following questions:
- What was the original intent for embarking on this trip? (to strengthen the new believers)
- What does this imply for our follow-up of new converts?
- What was the course of disagreement between Paul and Barnabas? (whether or not to take John Mark along again)
- What was the outcome of the dispute? (Paul and Barnabas parted company, Paul taking Silas with him, and Barnabas going to Cyprus with John Mark)
- Is this an example of how we are to settle such disputes, or of how the best of relationships can be disrupted? (It shows how the best of relationships can be disrupted.)

Paul's Third Missionary Journey (18:23—21:16)
Instruct the group to open their Bibles to Acts 18:23. Note that at this point Paul left Antioch once more to travel and share the gospel. Use the map to trace the progress of the third missionary journey. When you reach Ephesus ask the group, What significant facts did you learn about Paul's ministry at Ephesus? (The three-year visit to Ephesus represented the longest stay at a single location in Paul's ministry.)

Note for the group that Christianity spread so rapidly in Ephesus that those involved in sorcery burned their occult literature, and sales of shrines of the goddess Artemis dropped. Ask the group these questions:
- What group engaged in a protest of Paul's ministry? Why?

- Can you think of a New Testament verse that characterizes what happened at Ephesus? (Gal. 5:17)
- Did Paul purposely generate conflict with the silversmiths' guild or did he just do his work of evangelism?
- Can you think of modern circumstances in which the moral and spiritual demands of the gospel threaten the economic base of some businesses?
- How should we respond to the existence of such enterprises?
- What response should we expect from the ungodly when their way of life is threatened?

Briefly review for the group the events leading up to Paul being taken prisoner and sent to Rome for trial.

Paul's Voyage to Rome (27:1-44)

Call for the report on Paul's voyage to Rome. Ask the following questions as you discuss this passage.
- What was the name of the centurion in charge of Paul? (Julius)
- Why did Paul advise the group against traveling? (He knew the winter storms were coming.)
- How was the decision reached to go ahead and sail? (After a conference with the pilot, ship owner, and the group, they decided to sail.)
- What happened to establish Paul's credibility with the centurion? (His advice about the storm came true.)
- How did God speak in the midst of this crisis? (An angel told him they would all be spared.)
- How did Julius respond to Paul's advice after this point? (He listened and did exactly as he said.)
- How many people were on board the ship? (276)
- How many were lost in the shipwreck? (none)

After the discussion of the shipwreck narrative, ask the group the following questions:
- Can you think of other instances in which the majority ruled, only to bring later hardship or loss on everyone? (the account of the faithless spies: Numbers 13)
- What does this say to us about seeking God's will as we make decisions?

As time permits, lead the group to discuss the things God said to them during the week as they studied.

CONCLUSION—10 MINUTES

Preview next week's materials. Ask members to look at the unit overview appearing at the beginning of unit 9. Next week they will begin studying The Writings of Paul with a close look at the Book of Romans.

After the Session

1. Carefully evaluate the effectiveness of the session. Use the questions that appear on page 11 in the course administrative plan to guide your evaluation.

2. Save any materials you have developed for use in future groups of *Step by Step Through the New Testament*.

3. Immediately begin your preparations for next week's session.

4. Pray for the group. This week you will want to pray for their continued growth in the conviction that people who do not know Christ are truly separated from the grace and goodness of God, and they need Jesus' saving presence in their lives.

GROUP SESSION 9

The Writings of Paul Part 1 (Romans)

SESSION GOALS

 At the conclusion of this session members will be able to:

1. List characteristics of Paul's personality.
2. Name the three sources Paul used in writing letters.
3. Explain the arrangement of Paul's letters to churches and individuals.
4. Name the significant themes and words appearing in the Book of Romans.
5. State in their own words the meaning of select verses from the Book of Romans.

Before the Session

❑ 1. Study carefully unit 9 and complete all learning activities. Review the group session goals above.

❑ 2. Pray for God's guidance as you prepare for this group session. Pray specifically for each member of your group.

❑ 3. Read through "During the Session." You may not have time in the session to cover all the questions in your Leader Guide. Ask God to guide you to the questions He wants discussed with the group. Decide on the amount of time to allow for each segment of the Bible study. Write in the margin of your Leader Guide the time you want each segment to begin.

❑ 4. Reproduce one copy of the unit review quiz for each member.

During the Session

Part I
OPENING ACTIVITIES—20 MINUTES

1. Welcome members and begin with prayer. (5 mins.)

2. Distribute and have members complete the unit review quiz. When they have finished, lead a discussion of their answers. (10 mins.) Quiz answers: 1-F, 2-E, 3-G, 4-I, 5-B, 6-A, 7-J, 8-H, 9-D.

Part II
BIBLE STUDY AND GROUP DISCUSSION—50 MINUTES

The Man Paul
Have the group describe Paul's personality. (Refer the group as needed to pp. 138-39 in the member book.)

Ask the group to briefly recall the chronology of Paul's life. (born in Tarsus, absorbed Greek culture, Jew from the tribe of Benjamin and a Roman citizen, studied under Gamaliel, zeal for law, persecution of Christians)

The Pauline Letters: Their Characteristics, Structure, and Arrangement
As you begin the discussion of the writings of Paul, ask the group, How many books of the New Testament are attributed directly to Paul? (13) Beginning with Romans, have them recall the names of the letters written by Paul.

Ask the following questions as you construct a chronology of the writing of Paul's letters. (If necessary, refer the group to the box at the bottom of p. 144).
- Which of Paul's letters was written on his first missionary journey? (Galatians)
- Which letters were written on the second missionary journey? (Thessalonians)
- Which letters were written on the third missionary journey? (1 and 2 Corinthians and Romans)

- Which letters were written after his release? (1 Timothy and Titus)
- Which letter was written during his second imprisonment? (2 Timothy)
- Why are the letters to Timothy and Titus called the pastoral epistles? (They were addressed to those men, pastors of churches, dealing with church problems.)

Read or quote 2 Timothy 3:16-17. Then ask the following questions:
- What four things did Paul say the Scriptures are useful for? (teaching, rebuking, correcting, training in righteousness)
- Which other apostle mentioned Paul's writings being Scripture? (Peter: 2 Peter 3:16)
- What did you learn about the arrangement of Paul's letters in our English Bible? (Arranged in order of length)
- How many of Paul's letters were to churches? (9)
- How many of Paul's letters were to individuals? (4)

The Church at Rome

Have the group recall the following as you begin the Bible study. You may use the following questions.
- When did the Emperor Claudius ban Jews from Rome? (A.D. 49-50, see Acts 18:2)
- Why were they banned? (The Roman writer Suetonius stated they were expelled because of the unrest among the Jews due to a certain "Chrestus." Most biblical scholars think the similarity between "Chrestus" and "Christus" (Christ) indicates there was a conflict between believing and unbelieving Jews.)
- What does the expulsion of the Jews at this early date mean? (Christianity was already in Rome before the middle of the first century.)

Background to the Book of Romans

Ask the following questions:
- What is the general outline of the Book of Romans? (Refer to p. 149 as necessary for the outline.)
- What is the dominant theme in this book? (salvation through faith in Jesus Christ)
- What was the purpose of Romans? (to prepare the people for Paul's first visit there)
- What evidence did you see that indicates the Book of Romans was written to a congregation Paul had not founded himself?

The Message of Romans

Instruct the group to open their Bibles to Romans 1 as you begin the discussion. Use the following questions as you discuss the book:
- What three words can be used to state the theme of Romans? (salvation, righteousness, and faith)
- How are these words to be understood?
    - Salvation—deliverance from past penalty of sin, present power of sin, and future presence of sin.
    - Righteousness—both a conformity to an unchanging standard and a gift of right standing with God by faith in Jesus Christ.
    - Faith—a response of the whole person to God's revelation in Christ. It included the understanding of the intellect, the depth of the emotions, and the commitment of the will.

Ask, What did you find to be the meaning of the terms, *atonement, redemption,* and *justification?*

Atonement (3:25) teaches that the blood of Christ has met the demands of a holy God to punish sin, and turned aside God's wrath against us.

Redemption (3:24) is a term borrowed from the practice of slavery in that day. It teaches that Christ has paid the price to purchase freedom for believers from the penalty and practice of sin.

Justification (3:24) teaches that in Christ each believer is declared righteous by God when the believer puts his faith in Jesus Christ.

Ask, How were believers in the Old Testament saved? (They were saved just like we are: through faith.) There is a chance some member may argue the Old Testament saints were saved by sacrifice.

Refer the group to the section about Abraham on page 151. Note that no sacrifice a person could offer had saving effect apart from faith in God. The sacrifice was an act of obedience because of their faith. Paul clearly indicates that Abraham was saved (made righteous) by his faith. Finally, mention to the group that if they have not already been involved, the LIFE course *Step by Step Through the Old Testament* will help them understand more about faith and the sacrificial system of the Jews.

God's Plan for Israel and the Gentiles (Rom. 9—11)

Refer the group to Romans 9:30—10:13. As you discuss the passage, ask the following questions:
- What were the names of the two groups of people discussed in this passage? (Jews and Gentiles)
- What were the two approaches to righteousness discussed in this passage? (faith versus works)
- What means has God chosen to provide righteousness? (faith in Christ)
- What does it mean to "believe in your heart?" (to make a personal, willing commitment of your entire life to Christ)
- What must you believe in your heart to be saved? (that Jesus was raised from the dead and is in fact the Lord)
- What does it mean to confess with your mouth? (to agree with and verbally state the truth about Jesus)
- What must you confess with the mouth? (heart belief in Jesus' saving work and surrender to His Lordship)

God's Plan for Christian Living (Rom. 12:1—15:13)

Instruct the group to open their Bibles to Romans 12:1 as you begin the discussion. Ask the following questions as you discuss this passage:
- What is "the pattern of this world?" (thinking and acting in a manner that is ruled by the sin nature)
- How are we renewed in our minds? (through the renewal of the Holy Spirit and the retraining of our minds by the Word of God)
- Why is it necessary to be conformed to Christ and renewed in our minds before we can know God's will? (Answers to this will vary.)

Principles of Conscience (Romans 14)

Refer the group to Romans 14. Tell them these verses outline for God's people some "principles of conscience" that govern our personal behavior, our relationships with other believers, and how that affects our relationship with God. Assign the following verses to the members: 3, 7, 12, 13, 14, 15, 19. Instruct them to silently read their assigned verses. After a moment ask the group:
- What does verse 3 say about judging others?
- What does verse 7 say about our relationship to other believers?
- What does verse 12 say about our relationship with God?
- What does verse 13 say about our relationship to other believers?
- What does verse 14 say about the eating of certain foods? What else could "food" represent? (sports, places we go, activities we participate in, and so forth)
- What does verse 15 say about the effect of our actions on others?
- Does verse 19 mean we must make peace at the expense of moral principle? If not, then what does it mean to "make every effort to do what leads to peace and to mutual edification"?

As time permits, lead the group to discuss the things God said to them during the week as they studied.

CONCLUSION—10 MINUTES

Preview next week's materials. Have members look at the unit overview appearing at the beginning of unit 10. Next week they will continue studying the writings of Paul, covering 1 Corinthians through Ephesians.

After the Session

1. Carefully evaluate the effectiveness of the session. Use the questions that appear on page 11 in the course administrative plan to guide your evaluation.

2. Pray for the members of your group. This week you will want to pray for them to develop the maturity to discipline themselves and to live with a clear conscience before God.

GROUP SESSION 10 — The Writings of Paul Part 2 (1 Cor.—Eph.)

SESSION GOALS

At the conclusion of this session members will be able to:

1. State the purpose of each book covered in the unit.

2. Explain why the Books of Corinthians are valuable in the modern day church.

3. Give reasons for exercising godly church discipline in obedience to the Scriptures.

4. Explain why it is important to be equally yoked in the vital relationships of life.

5. Recall the works of the flesh and fruit of the Spirit.

Before the Session

❑ 1. Study carefully unit 10. Complete all learning activities. Review the group session goals above.
❑ 2. Pray for God's guidance as you prepare for this group session. Pray specifically for each member of your group.
❑ 3. Read through "During the Session." You may not have time in the session to cover all the questions in your Leader Guide. Ask God to guide you to the questions He wants discussed with the group. Decide on the amount of time to allow for each segment of the Bible study. Write in the margin of your Leader Guide the time you want each segment to begin.
❑ 4. Make each member a copy of the unit review quiz.
❑ 5. Optional: Choose four key statements or truths from the Scripture passages or from the member book to be discussed by the group during the session. Write them on a large piece of paper or poster board and hang them on the wall or hand them out at an appropriate time for the members to discuss. (You will need to decide where to include this activity in the session.)
❑ 6. Provide for refreshments if they are being served.

During the Session

Part I
OPENING ACTIVITIES—20 MINUTES

1. Welcome members and begin with prayer. (5 mins.)
2. Distribute and have members complete the unit review quiz. When they have finished, lead a discussion of their answers. (10 mins.) Quiz Answers: 1-F, 2-H, 3-A, 4-E, 5-G, 6-B, 7-D, 8-I, 9-C, 10-J.

Part II
BIBLE STUDY AND GROUP DISCUSSION—50 MINUTES

Give members time to review the introductory paragraphs on the unit page (p. 155). Have them close their books. Ask members to name the biblical books covered in this unit. Then have them state key words that remind them of each book.

Locate on the map the cities in which the churches existed that will be discussed in this unit.

The Background to the Corinthian Letters
Ask these questions to help members state the key facts about Corinth and the church there.
- What did you learn about Corinth? (Largest and most prosperous city of Greece, several hundred thousand population, located on an isthmus between northern Greece and the Peloponnesian Peninsula. Known for widespread immorality. The Acrocorinth rose 2000 feet above the city and was the setting for a temple dedicated to Aphrodite, the pagan goddess of love.)

- What occasion prompted the writing of 1 Corinthians? (Paul may have received reports about problems from friends in the church as well as an inquiry from Corinth requesting his advice and guidance on questions of interest to the church, 7:1)
- What were some of the problems the church was facing? (divisions over a variety of issues and severe problems of immorality in the congregation)
- What was the nature of the questions addressed to Paul? (marriage, Christian liberty, public worship, spiritual gifts, the resurrection, giving, stewardship)
- What words would you use to describe the church at Corinth?

First Corinthians

Instruct the group to open their Bibles to 1 Corinthians. As you begin the discussion ask, Why is 1 Corinthians valuable to us in our churches today? (It presents many vital truths dealing with the crucifixion and resurrection of Christ, and the role of the Holy Spirit in spiritual gifts. It provides principles for us to follow as we deal with problems in our own churches.)

Refer the group to 1 Corinthians 1:10-12. After they look over these verses, ask the following questions:
- Paul made what appeal to the Corinthians? (agree with one another and avoid divisions in the church)
- Who informed Paul of the problems? (members of the congregation from the household of Chloe)
- Say, The people of Chloe's household went on record as reporting the problems to Paul. What is your opinion about those of Chloe's household?

Mention that these persons were willing to admit reporting to Paul. Ask members to respond to that principle of accountability with the following questions.
- What would result in our (or any) church if people:
  - Only told what they were willing to be quoted on? (There would be less loose talk!)
  - Only listened to what they would be comfortable admitting in public? (There would be less indiscriminate listening.)
- Can you think of persons who have been hurt by indiscriminate conversation or by intentional gossip? (It is not necessary to name these persons.)
- How might someone of Chloe's integrity deal with those engaging in such destructive talk?

Note that the divisions were over who was the most significant leader. Ask,
- What did Paul indicate to be the problem with taking sides over human leadership?
- Does this mean not to support human leadership?
- How are we in our churches similar to Christians in the church at Corinth?

Refer the group to 1 Corinthians 2:1-5. Ask them:
- What misconceptions about qualifications of a minister existed in the minds of the Corinthians? (They focused on personality and worldly standing and viewed ministers as competitors with one another.)
- If other ministers and churches are not our competitors, who is? (Recreation, sports, laziness, lack of commitment, and other worldly pursuits are the real competitors for believers' time and resources.)
- What did Paul indicate to be the validation of a minister's qualifications? (a personal knowledge of the Lord Jesus, a message centered in the cross, the presence and power of the Holy Spirit, and reliance on the wisdom of God)

Read or quote 1 Corinthians 3:1-3 to the group. Ask:
- What does this passage indicate to be characteristics of an immature Christian? (worldliness, divisions, jealousy, and squabbling)
- What does this passage indicate to be characteristics of an immature church? (worldliness, divisions, jealousy, and squabbling)
- How does one move beyond such immature behavior and become a mature, fruitful disciple? (by laying aside the things of the flesh and obeying the teachings of the Scriptures)
- When does the "momentum" begin to turn in a godly direction in a congregation? (when a majority of the fellowship begins to mature and walk daily in the power of God)

Church Discipline: 1 Corinthians 5—6

Introduce the subject of church discipline to the group with the following questions.
- What do you think of when you think of church discipline? (Allow time for personal responses.)
- Do you know of a situation in which a Christian was restored by the exercise of godly discipline?

Ask the following questions:
- What was the nature of the moral problem mentioned in 1 Corinthians 5? (incest)
- How had the Corinthian church responded? (Apparently they were proud in the situation: see v. 2. Certainly they did nothing to correct it.)
- What should have been their response? (grief over the reality of the sin)
- How did Paul instruct them to respond? (expel the immoral member from their fellowship)
- Does the context of chapters 5 and 6 hint at the possibility of other types of moral problems in the church? (Yes. The strong possibility exists that other members of that congregation were involved in other types of immorality. See 1 Corinthians 6:9-20.)

Ask the group to respond to the following questions.
- Why did Paul command them to expel the person? (to indicate the disapproval of the church, to uphold God's honor and the integrity of the church in the community, and to protect the church from further harmful influences)
- What would be the effect on the person expelled? (the realization of the limits of acceptable behavior)
- What would be the effect on the church? (the assurance it had acted obediently, redemptively, and with integrity)
- What is the purpose of godly church discipline? (to act as a correction of unacceptable behavior, to redeem the life and testimony of the sinful member, and to uphold the honor of the Lord in the eyes of the world)
- Under what conditions could such a member be accepted back into the fellowship of the church? (on confession and repentance of the sin)

Principles of Conscience and Individual Rights: Chapter 8
Refer the group to the art work appearing in the margin of page 158. Have a member summarize chapter 8. Ask the following questions:
- What does the caption "limited liberty" mean to you?
- Why does the Scripture teach we are to voluntarily limit the exercise of our freedom? (to avoid placing a stumbling block in the path of another)
- What parallels do you see in the society at Corinth and the one in which we live?
- What are some areas in which we should limit ourselves to benefit those around us?
- Do you agree or disagree "we can make an idol of individual rights?"
- How did the author sum up the teaching of chapter 8? (If no one answers this, read the author's statements appearing on page 159, "He urged all of his readers to seek the glory of God and not merely their own individual rights and privileges [10:31].")

Spiritual Gifts
Refer the group to 1 Corinthians 12:4-11. After they have a moment to read the passage, ask the following questions:
- Who uses the gifts in the church? (God does: v. 6)
- Why are the gifts given? (for the good of all: v. 7)
- Who determines our spiritual gifts? (Holy Spirit: v. 11)

Note: The following resources are available to inform and train church members in the area of spiritual gifts.
- The LIFE discipleship training process MasterLife equips participants with a general background for understanding and using spiritual gifts in the body of Christ.

Paul's Second Letter to Corinth
Ask, when was 2 Corinthians written? (Around A.D. 56, approximately a year after the collection of the money for poor Jerusalem Christians).

Ask, Why was 2 Corinthians written? (Paul wanted to explain the greatness of the ministry God had given him; he appealed to the Corinthians to complete giving to the Jerusalem Christians; to defend his apostleship.) Refer the group to 2 Corinthians 6:14—7:16 in their Bibles, and to page 163 in their member's books. Ask,
- What did Paul mean by the command "do not be yoked together with unbelievers"?
- What do you think being "yoked together with unbelievers" means today?
- What is the motive or purpose behind being equally yoked in business, marriage, and so forth?
- What are some problems that can result from being unequally yoked?
- What are some benefits of being equally yoked?

The Book of Galatians

Ask, How was the term *Galatia* used? (*Galatia* was used in two different ways in the New Testament period: as an ethnic term and as reference to a political entity. As an ethnic term it referred to the area of central Asia Minor where people with Celtic background from Gaul came to live. The "political" Galatia included cities such as Pisidian Antioch, Iconium, Lystra, and Derbe.

Ask, Why was the Book of Galatians written? (Galatian Christians were in danger of following false teachers. Paul wrote to defend the gospel of salvation by grace through faith and to defend his ministry as an apostle.)

Ask, What statements did Paul make to defend his ministry? (Paul stated he received his gospel directly from God. He suggested no other apostles contributed to the content of his gospel. When he explained his gospel to friends, they accepted him and accredited the gospel he preached (2:1-10). He pointed out he was able to rebuke even Peter without having his ideas rejected.)

Refer the group to Galatians 5:16-26. Have the group recall from memory the works of the flesh. Next, have them recall the fruit of the spirit.

Refer the group to the art work in the left-hand lower margin of page 167, Ask, What does the picture say to you? (Interpretations may vary, but the message of the art work is that the fruit of the spirit is to be manifest in every area of our life.)

Ask, If your coworkers, employees, or employer were asked to label your life a type of fruit, which description would they choose? (fleshly or spiritual)

The Prison Epistles: Ephesians, Philippians, Colossians, Philemon

Ask the group to recall which letters of Paul are called the Prison Letters. After they name them ask why they are called by that term. (They were written while Paul was in prison in Rome.)

Say, this week we will discuss only Ephesians. The other three books will be covered in the next unit.

The Book of Ephesians

Have a member describe the city of Ephesus. (Include matters of location, culture, population, and the pagan temple of Artemis. The introduction to Ephesians appears at the bottom of p. 168 in the member's book.)

Briefly review Paul's ministry in Ephesus. Ask the group to recall:
 a. When Paul arrived in Ephesus. (His first visit was near the end of the second missionary journey: Acts 18:18-21. His second visit was on his third journey, at which time he remained there for around three years: Acts 19:1)
 b. The themes that are prominent in Ephesians. (See the member's book, pp. 169-70.)

As time permits, lead the group to discuss the things God said to them during the week as they studied.

CONCLUSION—10 MINUTES

1. Preview next week's materials. Ask members to look at the unit overview appearing at the beginning of unit 11 (p. 172). Next week they will be studying the final section on Paul's writings, covering the Books of Philippians—Titus.

After the Session

1. Carefully evaluate the effectiveness of the session. Use the questions that appear on page 11 in the course administrative plan to guide your evaluation.

2. Save any materials you have developed for use in future groups of *Step by Step Through the New Testament*.

3. Immediately begin your preparations for next week's session.

4. Pray for the group. This week you will want to pray for the members to attire themselves in the "full armor of God" as they face a society each day that is hostile to their faith in Christ.

GROUP SESSION 11
The Writings of Paul Part 3 (Phil.—Titus)

SESSION GOALS

At the conclusion of this session members will be able to:

1. Explain how adversity equips us to minister to others.

2. Explain why Paul was content in any and all circumstance.

3. Express a Christian response to dealing with disappointment.

4. State reasons why it is necessary to deal firmly with false doctrine.

Before the Session

❏ 1. Study carefully unit 11 and complete all learning activities. Review the group session goals above.
❏ 2. Pray for God's guidance as you prepare for this group session. Pray specifically for each member of your group.
❏ 3. Read through "During the Session." You may not have time in the session to cover all the questions in your Leader Guide. Ask God to guide you to the questions He wants discussed with the group. Decide on the amount of time to allow for each segment of the Bible study. Write in the margin of your Leader's Guide the time you want each segment to begin.
❏ 4. Make each member a copy of the unit review quiz.
❏ 5. Optional: Choose four key statements or truths from the Scripture passages or from the member book to be discussed by the group during the session. Write them on a large piece of paper or poster board and hang them on the wall or hand them out at an appropriate time for the members to discuss. (You will need to decide where to include this activity in the session.)
❏ 6. Provide for refreshments if they are being served during the break.

During the Session

Part I
OPENING ACTIVITIES—20 MINUTES

1. Welcome members and begin with prayer. (5 mins.)

2. Distribute and have members complete the unit review quiz. When they have finished, lead a discussion of their answers. (10 minutes) Quiz Answers: 1-B, 2-E, 3-H, 4-C, 5-A, 6-D, 7-G, 8-I, 9-F.

Part II
BIBLE STUDY AND GROUP DISCUSSION—50 MINUTES

Give the group a moment to look at the brief introduction to the books covered in this unit (p. 172). Have them close their books. Ask the group to state key words that identify the themes of each book. When finished, locate on the map on page 121 the cities and churches that will be discussed in this unit.

The Book of Philippians
Have the group recall the background of Paul's ministry at Philippi (see Acts 16:12-40; 2-:1-2). Ask the group to recall the significance of the founding of that church. (It was the first church on the European continent.)

Ask these questions as you begin the Bible study.
- What themes are prominent in this book? (joy, unity)
- Why was the book written? (to express Paul's gratitude for the gift they had sent him and to warn

them against divisiveness and the influence of the Judaizers)
- What was the composition of the Philippian church? (primarily Gentile)

Paul in Prison: Contentment in Adverse Circumstances

If it has not been mentioned already in the session, remind the group that Paul was in prison when he wrote this letter. Read Philippians 4:10-11 to the group. Ask, Why, while in prison, was Paul able to say that he was content in any and all circumstances? (because of his intimate personal relationship with Christ)

Ask the group to discuss what is necessary for a growing personal relationship with the Lord. As they address this subject, you may want to ask these questions:
- What role do the Scriptures have in our personal walk with Christ?
- What is the importance of our prayer life?
- Why is our fellowship with other believers vital to our walk with God?
- How does sharing our faith with others enable us to mature in the Lord?
- What type of service will maturing Christians be involved in?

Ask the group to recall the relationship between obedience and abiding that was studied in John's Gospel. (obedience is synonymous with abiding)

Growth Through Adversity

Note: Discuss the next series of questions in one of two ways. Determine ahead of time whether to address them as a group or by dividing into pairs and assigning one of the questions to each pair. If you choose the second option, allow pairs 5 minutes to discuss the questions, then call the group together for reports.

Lead the group to discuss how adversity helps one grow as a Christian. This series of questions is adapted from the "Guide to Praying in Faith" from *MasterLife: Discipleship Training* by Avery T. Willis, Jr. (Nashville: LifeWay Press, 1980). Discuss the following questions: How can God use adversity in my life as…
   a. a platform to demonstrate His power?
   b. a blessing from Him for which I did not ask?
   c. an opportunity to develop in me faith, love, patience, or some other character trait?
   d. an opportunity for me to develop a more effective prayer life?

Lead the group in a discussion of the personal response on page 174. As they are comfortable, allow them to share how their adversities have enable them to minister to others.

The Book of Colossians

Have the group recall the following information as you discuss Colossians.
   a. Who is thought to have founded the church at Colossae? (Epaphras)
   b. What theme is prominent in this book? (the Supremacy of Christ)
   c. Why was the book written? (First, Paul found in Colossae a heresy concerning Christ's person. Second, Paul emphasized the application of Christ's power for daily practice.)
   d. What was the composition of the Colossian church? (mostly Gentile)

Refer the group to Colossians 1:9-14 and to the activity at the bottom of page 176 in their books. Ask the members which two statements they would choose to have someone pray for them. As they are comfortable, allow them to state why they made particular choices.

Lead a brief prayer for those desires to be realized in the life of each member.

Ask the following questions:
- As you have studied the writings of Paul, what has struck you about the churches of the New Testament? (They are just like our churches today.)
- Since God dealt effectively with those problems through the inspired Scriptures and committed, obedient disciples, what does that say to us?
- If we are not experiencing the dynamic life of Christ seen in the Scriptures, what must take place for us to live in union with Christ?

Philemon

Have the group recall the following information as you discuss Philemon.

- What was Paul's relationship to Philemon? (Philemon had become a believer through Paul's ministry.)
- Why was Philemon written? (to intercede on behalf of Onesimus, a runaway slave who had become a believer)
- What is Philemon's theme? (worth of the individual)
- What is unique about this letter? (It is a personal letter to a friend about a personal matter. Also, it addressed indirectly the matter of slavery.)
- What was the meaning of Onesimus' name? (profitable)
- Does Paul hint to Philemon that Onesimus has now become profitable to him? (see v. 11)

As you discuss the circumstances of Philemon, ask,
- What words can you think of that might have expressed how Philemon felt when he discovered Onesimus was gone? (disappointment, joy, concern, anger, betrayal, grief, shock, relief, others)
- What do you think Philemon may have felt when he saw Onesimus enter his home with Tychicus?

Say, Put yourself in Philemon's place. What would be an appropriate Christian response to Onesimus' return?

Note the author's statement appearing at the top of page 179: "His (Paul's) description of the relationship between Philemon and Onesimus as 'brothers' sounded the death knell for slavery." Ask the group why that is a true statement. (Their response should reflect the conviction that once someone recognizes another as a brother in Christ it makes it impossible to legitimately abuse him or retain him as mere property.)

First Thessalonians
Have the group recall the background of Paul's ministry at Thessalonica (see Acts 17:1-9; 2-:1-3). Ask,
- What is the theme of 1 Thessalonians? (encouragement to the Christian)
- Why was 1 Thessalonians written? (to give guidance to young Christians who were in danger of being upset by false teaching, and to encourage them as they faced persecution)
- What was the composition of the church? (mostly Gentile)
- Why was Thessalonica significant? (It was an important naval center, a free city, and the capital of Macedonia. It was located on the Egnatian Way.)

Refer the group to the activity at the bottom of page 182. Ask,
- Do you agree that all statements except number 7 are true statements? Why or why not?
- Why is statement number 7 a false statement?
- What is the (fine) line between showing concern for one another and "minding one another's business"?

Second Thessalonians
Have members open their Bibles to 2 Thessalonians. Ask the following questions:
- When was 2 Thessalonians written?
- What was the nature of the misunderstanding that prompted Paul to write 2 Thessalonians? (Some members were confused about Christ's return.)
- What is the theme of 2 Thessalonians? (God's people stand corrected.)

Option: Group Discussion
Say, Would you agree or disagree that in some cases the business community is more redemptive than the church in dealing with problems?

Allow time for the group to respond. I would agree, because many companies will confront the issue, obtain help for the person, and salvage both the person and the relationship.

Say, The church functions today in a society that is as selfish and undisciplined as that of the first century A.D. Ask, In the midst of such a society, what would be the result for the church if it ...
- obeyed Christ in every way?
- supported and defended its leadership?
- disciplined its unruly or disobedient members in obedience to the Scriptures?
- stood firm for the integrity of the church, holding all its members accountable without partiality?

Emphasize to the group the need for churches to care enough for their members to teach and practice godly discipline. Read or quote Galatians 6:1 to the group. Lead the group in a brief prayer for the conviction and wisdom to function as a redemptive, healing body for all its membership.

The Pastoral Epistles: 1 and 2 Timothy, Titus
Engage the group in a general discussion about the pastoral epistles. Ask the following questions:
- Which letters are known as the Pastoral Letters?
- Why are these called the Pastoral letters?
- Why did Paul write these letters? (to help the leaders in the churches at Ephesus and Crete deal with problems of false teaching)

First Timothy
Instruct the group to open their Bibles to 1 Timothy. Ask the following questions:
- When was this letter written? (during Paul's release following his first Roman imprisonment)
- What was the probable date of the writing? (A.D. 63-65)
- Where was Timothy serving? (at Ephesus)
- Why did Paul write so forcefully to Timothy? (to help him overcome his hesitancy in dealing with the problems)

Discuss 1 Timothy 3:1-13 by asking:
- Is there a "triple standard" for moral and ethical behavior taught here? (One standard for pastors, a second for deacons, a third for "ordinary" members. The obvious answer is "no." But sometimes we practice it that way.
- What is lost in our understanding of this passage if the application is limited only to the offices of the pastor and deacon? (The application to other leaders in the church is lost. In context it spoke of pastors and deacons. In principle it speaks to every church leader.)

Titus
Instruct the group to open their Bibles to Titus. Have the group recall the following from their study.
- When was this book written? (during the same period as 1 Timothy—during Paul's release following his first Roman imprisonment)
- Why was Titus left on Crete? (to deal with church problems and false teachers)

Refer the group to Titus 1:10—2:1. Note that Paul's instruction called for a strong response from Titus. Ask, what is the difference in being a strong leader and being an overbearing one?

Refer the group to the paired statements on pages 188-89. Beginning with the second part, lead the group in a discussion of pairs 2 through 4. Be sure they understand why the correct statements are true.

Second Timothy
Have the group recall the following information as you study this section.
- When was 2 Timothy written? (during Paul's second and final imprisonment)
- Why do we believe it was his last letter? (Verses in chap. 4 indicate Paul believed his death was near.)

Refer the group to 2 Timothy 2:14-19 and to the personal response on page 187. Ask them to discuss these questions:
- What is the difference in a healthy examination of what one believes and a destructive discussion of ideas?
- How has your faith grown as you have studied *Step by Step Through the New Testament*?

As time permits, lead the group to discuss the things God said to them during the week as they studied.

CONCLUSION—10 MINUTES
1. Preview next week's materials. Ask members to look at the unit overview appearing at the beginning of unit 12 on page 190. Next week they will be studying the General Letters: Hebrews; James; 1 and 2 Peter; 1, 2, and 3 John; and Jude.
2. Optional: Assign a member to each of the general epistles. Have the member be prepared to answer the factual questions about the assigned book.

After the Session

1. Carefully evaluate the effectiveness of the session. Use the questions that appear on page 11 in the course administrative plan to guide your evaluation.
2. Save any materials you have developed for use in future groups of *Step by Step Through the New Testament*.
3. Begin your preparations for next week's session.
4. Pray for the members to have the knowledge to discern teaching that is not true to the Scriptures.

GROUP SESSION 12 The General Letters

SESSION GOALS

At the conclusion of this session members will be able to:

1. Explain why Hebrews was written and state its theme.

2. Describe the theme and emphasis of James.

3. Identify in 1 and 2 Peter the various ways Christians witness to the world.

4. List from John's letters the evidences of true faith, and explain how to walk in truth.

5. Explain the importance of contending for the faith as emphasized in the Book of Jude.

Before the Session

❏ 1. Study carefully unit 12 and complete all learning activities. Review the group session goals.

❏ 2. Pray for God's guidance as you prepare for this group session. Pray specifically for each member of your group by name.

❏ 3. Read "During the Session." You may not have time to cover all the questions in your Leader Guide. Ask God to guide you to the questions He wants discussed with the group. Decide on the amount of time to allow for each segment of the Bible study. Write in the margin of your Leader Guide the time you want each segment to begin.

❏ 4. Gather copies of the unit review quiz and other materials as needed to conduct the session.

❏ 5. Optional: Assign five members of the group to present an introduction and give a summary of Hebrews, James, 1 and 2 Peter, 1, 2, and 3 John, and Jude (no more than three minutes each).

❏ 6. Finalize plans for the closing session so you can share them at the conclusion of this session.

❏ 7. Provide for refreshments if they are to be served during the break.

During the Session

Part I
OPENING ACTIVITIES—15 MINUTES

1. Welcome members and begin with prayer. (5 mins.)

2. Distribute and have members complete the unit review quiz. When they have finished, lead a discussion of their answers. (10 mins.) Quiz Answers: A:b; B:1-D; 2-B; 3-A; 4-H; 5-E; 6-G; 7-C; 8-F.

Part II
BIBLE STUDY AND GROUP DISCUSSION—50 MINUTES

The Book of Hebrews
Have the group recall the following information and themes from Hebrews.

- Who were the readers of the letter to the Hebrews? (See p. 191.)

- Who might have been the author? Why do you think so? (See p. 191.)

- When was Hebrews written? (See p. 192.)

- Why was Hebrews written? (See p. 192.)

- Is an emphasis on this theme needed today?

- Hebrews mentions persecution for one's belief. Can you cite instances in which believers are being persecuted today?

- Hebrews mentions falling away from one's profession of Jesus Christ. How are people tempted to back away from their profession in Jesus today?

- Hebrews teaches about the priesthood of Christ. How does this emphasis apply today? (Heb. 4:14-16.)

- How does the emphasis on faith in chapter 11 apply today?

- How does the emphasis on hardship in chapter 12 apply today?

- How does the emphasis on church life in chapter 13 apply today?

- How does the passage in 13:5-6 on the love of money apply today?

- Optional: Call on the member assigned to give an introduction and summary of Hebrews. (3 minutes) Allow ample time for the group to discuss and respond to this report.

The Book of James
Have the group recall the following information and themes from James.

- Which James wrote this letter? Why do you think so? (See p. 197.)

- When was James written? Why do you think so? (See p. 197.)

- Were the readers of James Jewish or Gentile? (See p. 197.)

- Why was James written? (See p. 198.)

- What is the theme of James? (See p. 199.)

- Is an emphasis on this theme needed today?

- What are three evidences of spiritual need among the readers? (faith without works, partiality to rich, wrong use of tongue, worldly ways, arrogant attitude, others)

- Optional: Call on the member assigned to give an introduction and summary of James. (3 minutes) Allow ample time for the group to discuss and respond to this report.

The Books of 1 and 2 Peter
Have the group recall the following information and themes from 1 and 2 Peter.

- Were the readers of 1 and 2 Peter Jewish or Gentile? (p. 201)

- Why was 1 Peter written? (p. 201)

- List three ways Peter said Christians could witness to the world. (by holy living, by the way they endured unjust suffering, by a proper relationship to society, by demonstrating godliness in the home, and so on)

- What did Peter say about church leaders? (p. 202)

- Why was 2 Peter written? (p. 202)

- Do false teachers exist today?

- Why does the thought of Christ's return frighten some people? Should Christ's return frighten Christians or fill us with joy?

- Optional: Call on the member assigned to give an introduction and summary of 1 and 2 Peter. (3 minutes) Allow ample time for the group to discuss and respond to this report.

The Books of 1, 2, and 3 John
- What did the heresy *Gnosticism* teach? (p. 204)

- Why was Gnosticism a threat to the Christian faith? (See p. 204.)

- Why did John write his first letter? (See p. 205.)

- What are three evidences of true faith? (walking in the Light, living in obedience and love; a correct view of Christ, love for others, turning from the world, recognition of and repudiation of false teaching, others)

- Why did John write his second letter?

- According to 2 John is it important to believe sound doctrine? (See p. 206.)

- Why did John write his third letter?

- According to 3 John what attitude are church members to exhibit? (See p. 206.)

- Optional: Call on the member assigned to give an introduction and summary of 1, 2, and 3 John. (3 minutes) Allow ample time for the group to discuss and respond to this report.

The Book of Jude
Have the group recall the following information and themes from Jude.

- Explain the importance of contending for the faith.

- Have the group recall the following information and themes from the Book of Jude
  a. Was Jude related to Jesus? (See p. 207.)
  b. Why did Jude write his letter? (See p. 207.)
  c. According to Jude 1:3, did it seem Jude enjoyed arguing and fighting? (No, but sometimes it is necessary to stand up for our faith in Christ.)
  d. List three truths Jude presented about false teachers. (deserving divine judgment, arrogant, corrupt ways, self-willed, doomed to future punishment)

- Optional: Call on the member assigned to give an introduction and summary of Jude. (3 minutes) Allow ample time for the group to discuss and respond to this report.

CONCLUSION—10 MINUTES

1. Preview next week's materials. Ask members to look at the unit overview appearing at the beginning of unit 13 on page 209. Next week they will be studying the Book of Revelation.

2. Give the members the following prayer assignment for the coming week, As you complete the final unit, ask God for the names of five persons who might be enlisted for the next class of *Step by Step Through the New Testament*. Ask them to write those names and bring them to you.

3. If you are planning a fellowship or some other special meeting for session 13, finalize those plans with the members at this time.

4. You may wish to announce that you will duplicate the Course Credit Request Form (p. 223) so members will not need to mar their books.

After the Session

1. Carefully evaluate the effectiveness of the session. Use the questions that appear on page 11 in the course administrative plan to guide your evaluation.

2. Save materials you have developed for use in future groups of *Step by Step Through the New Testament*.

3. Begin your preparations for next week's session.

4. Pray for the group. This week you will want to pray for a feeling of satisfaction and fulfillment for the members as they complete the final unit of *Step by Step Through the New Testament*.

GROUP SESSION 13 The Book of Revelation

SESSION GOALS

At the conclusion of this session members will be able to:

1. Explain the meaning of the word *revelation* and the purpose of the book.

2. Interpret various views people hold about the Book of Revelation.

3. Express the theme and the four visions of Revelation.

4. Describe the reign of Christ and the eternal blessing of heaven.

5. Testify to an expectancy for the coming of the Lord Jesus Christ.

Before the Session

❑ 1. Study carefully unit 13. Complete all learning activities. Review the group session goals above.

❑ 2. Pray for God's guidance as you prepare for this group session. Pray specifically for each member.

❑ 3. Read through "During the Session." You may not have time in the session to cover all the questions in your Leader Guide. Ask God to guide you to the questions He wants discussed with the group. Decide how much time to allow for each segment. Write in the Leader Guide the time you want each segment to begin.

❑ 4. Gather copies of the unit review quiz and enough three-by-five-inch cards to give each member one.

❑ 5. Contact your host if you are meeting in a home to make certain all is in order for the session. If the host needs assistance, enlist group members to help you with necessary preparations.

❑ 6. You may wish to duplicate the Christian Growth Study Plan Credit Request Form so members will not need to tear the page from their books.

During the Session

Part I
OPENING ACTIVITIES—20 MINUTES

1. Welcome members and begin with prayer (5 mins.)

2. Distribute and have members complete the unit review quiz. When they have finished, lead a discussion of their answers. (10 mins.) Quiz Answers: A: 1-D, 2-C, 3-A, 4-B; B: 1-B, 2-C, 3-A, 4-A.

Part II
BIBLE STUDY AND GROUP DISCUSSION—50 MINUTES

The Book of Revelation
As you begin, have the members turn to page 209 in their member's book and fill in the names of the books of the New Testament in order in the spaces provided.

Introductory Matters
When the members have completed this activity, instruct them to turn to the Book of Revelation in their Bibles. Ask the group these thought-provoking questions as you begin the Bible study (allow time for minimal responses; you can speed up responses by referring to pages listed from the member's book, and having them turn in their Bibles to the Scriptures cited). (10 minutes)

- Why are people afraid of the Book of Revelation?
- Why should we be eager to study Revelation? (See p. 209.)
- What kind of writing is Revelation? (p. 211)
- What are some special features of Revelation? (pp. 211-12)

Various Interpretations and Millennial Views

Assign group members to two buzz groups, separating husbands and wives.

Have Group A turn to pages 212-213 and discuss the four major approaches to interpreting. Designate one member as a reporter. (10 mins.)

Have Group B turn to page 213 and discuss the four millennial views. Designate one member as a reporter. (10 mins.)

Call the groups together and hear the two reports, allowing ample time for discussion. (10 mins.)

Ask, Does it matter what a Christian believes about the Book of Revelation? Give time for responses.

Ask, Does it matter what a Christian believes about the Lord's coming? Give time for responses. Be sure that the reality and importance of Jesus' promise to return is emphasized and stress that it is a blessed hope for Christians (Titus 2:13).

Four Visions of Revelation

Discuss the four visions of Revelation using the following questions (20 mins. See p. 214 for visions and Scriptures):

- How does each vision relate to the theme of Revelation?
- How would this book encourage first-century believers?
- How does Revelation encourage believers today?
- What does the word *signified* (v. 1) mean? Discuss the literal, yet symbolic, nature of Revelation (p. 215).

Christ Strengthening the Churches (Chapters 1—3)

Discuss the first vision. Ask, Are these churches all alike, or do they have differences? (They are all different. For example, compare Smyrna, Philadelphia, and Laodicea.) Have members turn to the map on page 209. Point out the close proximity of the churches.

Discuss the following points for each of the seven churches.
- Christ's comments concerning each church
- Christ's criticism concerning some churches
- Christ's commendation of some churches
- Christ's challenge to each church

Christ's Judgment on Sin (Chapter 4—16)

Discuss John's second vision. Write "seals," "trumpets," and "bowls" on a chalkboard or newsprint. Point to each word in turn and ask, How does this word relate to God's judgment on the world? (See pp. 217-18, 220.) Ask, Will Christ's Church be on the earth during part or all of these judgments? (See p. 216.)

Discuss the interlude in chapters 12—14. Assign members who have not spoken yet (or have not spoken much) to express what the following creatures represent (they may look in their Bibles and on page 219 of the member's book):
- woman
- dragon
- beast from the sea
- beast from the earth

Ask, Are some of the judgments (seals, trumpets, bowls) more partial, and some more complete? (See p. 220.)

Christ's Victory Over Evil (Chapters 17—20)

Discuss John's third vision. Ask, What does the vision of consummation represent? (See p. 220.) Ask, What will happen when Jesus returns? (See pp. 220-21.)

Christ's Ultimate Triumph (Chapter 21:0—22:21)

Discuss John's final vision. Ask, What does the "new Jerusalem" represent? What are some of its characteristics? (See p. 221.) Ask, What is the most beautiful thought you have concerning heaven?

CONCLUSION—30 MINUTES

1. Take up the course credit request forms. Make certain they are filled out properly.
2. Pray together. Allow members to share requests they may want to surface. Close in sentence prayers around the circle. You wait and pray last. Ask the Lord to use the growth that has occurred in the group member's lives to honor and magnify His name in the church and community in which you all live.

Optional: Hand out a three-by-five-inch card to the members. Ask them to reflect for a few minutes on the things God has said to them over the past 13 sessions. Then, ask them to share with the group what they recorded. You also may want to use the following questions in this discussion:

- Who was the most notable character you studied?

- What was the most surprising thing you learned?

- What one truth has God been using to adjust your life to His will?

- How has God been using the spiritual growth you have experienced to enable you to serve Him more effectively?

After the Session

1. Carefully evaluate the effectiveness of the session. Use the questions that appear on page 11 in the course administrative plan to guide your evaluation.

2. Save any materials you have developed for use in future groups of *Step by Step Through the New Testament*.

3. Make contact with any members who expressed an interest in leading future groups of *Step by Step Through the New Testament*. Answer any questions they might have, and share with them your willingness to help and serve as a resource person to them should they accept this task.

4. Pray for the group. In your concluding personal prayer for them you will want to pray for their commitment to continue to abide in Christ and to walk daily with God in the light of His Word.

5. Make certain that the Christian Growth Study Plan forms are mailed to Christian Growth Study Plan; One LifeWay Plaza; Nashville, TN 37234-0117; or faxed to (615) 251-5067. Alert the person receiving your church mail to the diplomas' expected arrival. Be certain the members receive their diplomas and other recognition as appropriate.

Unit Review Quizzes

UNIT 1 REVIEW QUIZ

Match the name on the left with the correct answer on the right. Fill in the blank with the correct letter.

___ 1. A "reed" or "a standard of measure."
___ 2. Roman Ruler who was Caesar at the time of Christ's birth.
___ 3. Roman Ruler who was Caesar at the time of Christ's death.
___ 4. Jewish group that believed in angels, demons, and a resurrection.
___ 5. Jewish sect that did not believe in angels, demons, or a resurrection.
___ 6. Jewish sect that lived monastic lives in the wilderness.
___ 7. Herod who was in power at the time of Jesus' birth.
___ 8. Herod who lost his throne because of his misrule.
___ 9. Herod who murdered James the apostle and imprisoned Peter.
___ 10. Herod who heard Paul's defense.

A. Canon
B. Pharisees
C. Herod the Great
D. Herod Agrippa II
E. Herod Agrippa I
F. Essenes
G. Tiberius
H. Augustus
I. Sadducees
J. Archelaus

UNIT 2 REVIEW QUIZ

A. Match the statement on the left with the correct answer on the right. Fill in the blank with the correct letter.

___ 1. The beginning point for the Romans in calculating years.
___ 2. This monk recommended a change of calendars that was accepted.
___ 3. When the calendar was changed to match the monk's calculations.
___ 4. A. D. or Anno Domini.
___ 5. The number of years the monk erred in his calculations.
___ 6. This Gospel writer tells us Jesus was born prior to the death of Herod the Great.
___ 7. Probable date of Jesus' birth.
___ 8. Governor of Syria at the time of Jesus' birth.
___ 9. Caesar at the time of Jesus' birth.
___ 10. The accepted date for Jesus' death.

A. Matthew
B. The founding of the city of Rome.
C. 6-5 B.C.
D. Dionysius
E. Quirinius
F. Sixth Century A.D.
G. Augustus
H. In the year of our Lord
I. A.D. 29
J. Four

B. Be prepared to discuss the following question in the group session. Why is the dating of the time of Jesus' birth, ministry, death, and resurrection important?

UNIT 3 REVIEW QUIZ

Match the description of the five discourses in Matthew's Gospel with their references. Fill in the blank with the correct letter.

___ 1. The Sermon on the Mount
___ 2. Commission to the Twelve
___ 3. Parables of the Kingdom
___ 4. Humility and Forgiveness
___ 5. The Olivet Discourse

A. Chapters 24—25
B. Chapter 10
C. Chapters 5—7
D. Chapter 13
E. Chapter 18

UNIT 4 REVIEW QUIZ

Reconstruct the outline of Mark's Gospel by matching the descriptions on the left with the Scripture references on the right.

___ 1. Jesus' Early Ministry
___ 2. Jesus' Ministry in Galilee
___ 3. Jesus' Journey to Jerusalem
___ 4. Jesus' Final Week

A. Mark 10:1-52
B. Mark 2:1—9:50
C. Mark 11:1—16:20
D. Mark 1:1-45

UNIT 5 REVIEW QUIZ

Match the statements on the left with the correct Scripture on the right. Fill in the blank with the correct letter.

___ 1. Parable of the Persistent Widow
___ 2. Jesus' Final Journey to Jerusalem
___ 3. Parable of the Rich Man and Lazarus
___ 4. Jesus' Early Ministry and Preaching
___ 5. Parable of the Prodigal Son
___ 6. Parable of the Rich Fool
___ 7. Birth and Childhood of Jesus
___ 8. Parable of the Good Samaritan
___ 9. Jesus' Galilean Ministry
___ 10. Jesus' Final Week, Crucifixion, Resurrection, and Ascension

A. Luke 1:1—2:52
B. Luke 10:25-37
C. Luke 3:1—4:13
D. Luke 12:13-21
E. Luke 4:14—9:50
F. Luke 15:11-24
G. Luke 9:52—19:27
H. Luke 16:19-31
I. Luke 18:1-8
J. Luke 19:28—24:53

UNIT 6 REVIEW QUIZ

Match the Scripture passages on the left with the correct answer on the right. Fill in the blank with the correct letter.

___ 1. "The Word was with God."
___ 2. "The Word became flesh and made his dwelling among us."
___ 3. Changing of the water into wine.
___ 4. Feeding of the five thousand.
___ 5. The woman caught in sin.
___ 6. "I am the light of the world."
___ 7. Healing of the man born blind.
___ 8. "I am the resurrection and the life."
___ 9. The raising of Lazarus from the dead.
___ 10. The reinstatement of Simon Peter.

A. John 2:1-11
B. John 11:25
C. John 1:14
D. John 9:1-41
E. John 1:1
F. John 8:12
G. John 21:15-23
H. John 6:1-15
I. John 11:38-44
J. John 7:53—8:11

UNIT 7 REVIEW QUIZ

Match the statements on the left with the correct answers on the right. Fill in the blank with the correct letter.

___ 1. The theme of Acts.
___ 2. "You will be my witnesses."
___ 3. The Ascension of Jesus.
___ 4. Peter's Sermon at Pentecost.
___ 5. The coming of the Holy Spirit.
___ 6. Ananias and Sapphira.
___ 7. Authored the Book of Acts.
___ 8. He was a friend to the author of Acts.
___ 9. He sought to purchase the power of God.
___ 10. He shared the gospel in the desert and in Samaria.

A. Philip
B. Theophilus
C. Acts 5:1-11
D. Acts 2:14-40
E. Acts 1:8
F. God's Holy Spirit spreads the gospel
G. Acts 1:1-11
H. Acts 2:1-13
I. Luke
J. Simon the Sorcerer

UNIT 8 REVIEW QUIZ

Match the description on the left with the correct answer on the right. Fill in the blanks with the correct letter.

___ 1. Prayed for Paul to receive his sight.
___ 2. Helped Paul gain entrance to the church at Jerusalem.
___ 3. A tanner who lived by the sea in Joppa.
___ 4. Shared the gospel with the centurion at Caesarea.
___ 5. First Gentile convert.
___ 6. First known church to formally send out missionaries.
___ 7. He and Paul were set aside for the first missionary journey.
___ 8. Started journey with Paul and Barnabas but later turned back.
___ 9. Paul stayed the longest period of time (nearly 3 years) in this city.
___ 10. Accompanied Paul to Rome.

A. John Mark
B. Simon Peter
C. Cornelius
D. Ephesus
E. Ananias
F. Simon
G. Antioch
H. Luke
I. Barnabas

UNIT 9 REVIEW QUIZ

Match the statements on the left with the correct name on the right. Fill in the blank with the correct letter.

___ 1. Paul's birthplace.
___ 2. Paul's conversion.
___ 3. Paul spent three years here rethinking his theology.
___ 4. "Be transformed by the renewing of your mind."
___ 5. "Each of us will give an account of himself to God."
___ 6. This man spoke of Paul's writings as Scripture.
___ 7. This emperor banned the Jews from Rome in A.D. 49-50.
___ 8. This Roman writer indicated the expulsion of the Jews was for religious reasons.
___ 9. This passage give the key verses of Romans.

A. Peter
B. Romans 14:12
C. Claudius
D. Romans 1:16-17
E. On the road to Damascus
F. Tarsus
G. Arabia and Damascus
H. Suetonius
I. Romans 12:2

UNIT 10 REVIEW QUIZ

Match the statements on the left with the correct answer on the right. Fill in the blank with the correct letter.

___ 1. Members from this household informed Paul of the Corinthian problems.
___ 2. Site of the pagan temple dedicated to Aphrodite.
___ 3. The name of Corinth.
___ 4. Letter of Paul that addresses problems of moral and theological failure.
___ 5. Letter of Paul that reminds us God's grace is all sufficient in our lives.
___ 6. Letter of Paul that defends the doctrine of salvation by grace through faith.
___ 7. Letter written in prison and emphasizes the church as the body of Christ.
___ 8. Pagan temple staffed by cult prostitutes.
___ 9. Scriptures in 1 Corinthians that address church discipline.
___ 10. Scriptures in 1 Corinthians relating to spiritual gifts in the body of Christ.

A. Synonymous with living an immoral lifestyle
B. Galatians
C. 1 Corinthians 5
D. Ephesians
E. 1 Corinthians
F. Chloe
G. 2 Corinthians
H. Acrocorinth
I. Aphrodite
J. 1 Corinthians 12—14

UNIT 11 REVIEW QUIZ

Match the statement on the left with the correct name on the right. Fill in the blank with the correct letter.

___ 1. Church that ministered to Paul while he was in prison.
___ 2. Paul's letter emphasizing the supremacy of Christ.
___ 3. This letter was the shortest and most personal of Paul's letters.
___ 4. Church that misunderstood the doctrine of the Lord's return.
___ 5. He was instructed to deal directly with problems at Ephesus.
___ 6. The young pastor left on Crete to deal with false teachers.
___ 7. The Prison Letters.
___ 8. The Pastoral Letters.
___ 9. Accompanied Tychicus to carry a letter to Philemon.

A. Timothy
B. Church at Philippi
C. Thessalonica
D. Titus
E. Colossians
F. Onesimus
G. Ephesians, Philippians, Colossians, Philemon
H. Philemon
I. 1 and 2 Timothy, Titus

UNIT 12 REVIEW QUIZ

A. Choose the correct ending to make a true statement. Check the correct box.

The General Letters:
❏ relate to no specific doctrines.
❏ have no specific destinations.
❏ have no specific authors.

B. Match the statements on the left with the correct book on the right. Fill in the blank with the correct letter.

___ 1. Explained the Day of the Lord.
___ 2. Stressed the control of the tongue.
___ 3. Emphasized the superiority of Christ.
___ 4. Urged readers to contend for the faith.
___ 5. Three tests of genuine Christian faith.
___ 6. Problem of a dictatorial leader.
___ 7. God's people witness through suffering.
___ 8. Theme is Walking in Truth

A. Hebrews
B. James
C. 1 Peter
D. 2 Peter
E. 1 John
F. 2 John
G. 3 John
H. Jude

UNIT 13 REVIEW QUIZ

A. Match John's four visions with the correct Scriptures. Fill in the blank with the correct letter.

___ 1. Christ's ultimate triumph.
___ 2. Christ's victory over evil.
___ 3. The glorified Christ strengthening His churches.
___ 4. Christ's judgment on sin.

A. Revelation 1:1—3.22
B. Revelation 4:1—16:21
C. Revelation 17:1—21:8
D. Revelation 21:9—22:21

B. Match the four millennial views with the summaries. Fill in the blank with the correct letter.

___ 1. Postmillennialism.
___ 2. Amillennialism.
___ 3. Historical Premillennialism.
___ 4. Dispensational Premillennialism

A. Christ brings millennium
B. Church brings millennium
C. No literal millennium on earth